PENGUIN CLASSICS

THE COMMUNIST MANIFESTO

KARL MARX was born at Trier in 1818 of a German-Jewish family which had been converted to Christianity. As a student at Bonn and Berlin he was influenced by Hegel's theory of the Dialectic, but he later reacted against the overt idealism of Hegel's system and found himself in sympathy with the exiled German socialists. *The Communist Manifesto* (which was composed in close collaboration with his friend Engels) was written in some haste in Brussels for the Communist League. After taking an active but ineffectual part in the revolutions of 1848, Marx fled to London, where he and his family lived in a poverty which was made bearable only by Engels's generous financial help. For some years he was London correspondent for a New York newspaper, but he spent most of his time in the British Museum researching into the class struggle and the economic laws underlying social progress. The first volume of his great work, *Das Kapital*, was published in 1867. His other works include *The Poverty of Philosophy*, *Theories of Surplus Value*, *The German Ideology* and *A Contribution to the Critique of Political Economy*. Marx lived in exile in London until his death in 1883.

FRIEDRICH ENGELS was born in Germany in 1820, the son of a textile manufacturer. After his military training in Berlin he became Manchester agent of his father's business, and soon became immersed in Chartism and the problems of the urban proletariat newly created by the industrial revolution. In 1844 he wrote his famous *Condition of the Working Classes in England*, and by 1848 he was a firm friend of Marx. Their ideas were incorporated into *The Communist Manifesto*, although the writing of the *Manifesto* itself was solely Marx's work. Engels provided Marx with money, and after 1870 spent all his time assisting him in his research. After Marx's death Engels continued his work on *Das Kapital*, and completed it in 1894, a year before his own death. He also wrote *The Peasant War in Germany*, *The Origin of the Family*, and *Socialism, Utopian and Scientific*.

A J P TAYLOR was an Honorary Fellow of Magdalen College, Oxford. His many books include *The Origins of the Second World War*, *The Habsburg Monarchy*, *The First World*

War: An Illustrated History, English History 1914–1945, Europe: Grandeur and Decline, Beaverbrook, The War Lords, Essays in English History, a collection of essays entitled *Politicians, Socialism and Historians* and a volume of autobiography entitled *A Personal History, An Old Man's Diary* and *How Wars End*. He died in 1990.

KARL MARX
FRIEDRICH ENGELS

THE COMMUNIST MANIFESTO

WITH AN INTRODUCTION AND NOTES
BY
A J P. TAYLOR

PENGUIN BOOKS

PENGUIN BOOKS

Published by the Penguin Group
Penguin Books Ltd, 27 Wrights Lane, London W8 5TZ, England
Penguin Putnam Inc., 375 Hudson Street, New York, New York 10014, USA
Penguin Books Australia Ltd, Ringwood, Victoria, Australia
Penguin Books Canada Ltd, 10 Alcorn Avenue, Toronto, Ontario, Canada M4V 3B2
Penguin Books (NZ) Ltd, Private Bag 102902, NSMC, Auckland, New Zealand

Penguin Books Ltd, Registered Offices: Harmondsworth, Middlesex, England

This translation, by Samuel Moore, first published 1888
Published with Introduction and Notes in Penguin Books 1967
Reprinted in Penguin Classics 1985
23

Introduction and Notes copyright © A. J. P. Taylor, 1967
All rights reserved

Printed in England by Clays Ltd, St Ives plc
Set in Intertype Times

Contents

Introduction

THIS work – tract or pamphlet rather than book – is deceptively slight in character and appearance. It is very short: a mere twelve thousand words, often less than the various introductions with which its re-publication has usually been accompanied. Its argument is simple, seeming to follow inevitably from the early sentence: 'The history of all hitherto existing society is the history of class struggles.' Karl Marx wrote it in six weeks or so with little time for deliberation or revision. No work has been more spontaneous and, at the same time, more final. Though Marx wrote a great deal later and added much by way of refinement or development to the outline which he had drawn here, *The Communist Manifesto* contains the essential doctrines of the outlook known as Marxism. As such, it takes first place, along with the *Origin of Species*, among the intellectual documents of the nineteenth century. Thanks to *The Communist Manifesto,* everyone thinks differently about politics and society, when he thinks at all. More than this, Marxism has become the accepted creed or religion for countless millions of mankind, and *The Communist Manifesto* must be counted as a holy book, in the same class as the Bible or the Koran. Nearly every sentence is a sacred text, quoted or acted on by devotees, who often no doubt do not know the source of their belief.

Few people foresaw this when the first thousand or so copies of the original German text were run off a London press in February 1848. Only Marx and his friend Engels regarded it as a document of any importance, and it passed unnoticed during the turmoil of the 1848 revolutions. Later events were to justify Marx's self-confidence. He was just under thirty when he wrote the *Manifesto*. Engels, who contributed some of the ideas, was a couple of years younger. Both had considerable experience in radical and revolutionary journalism. Both had written substantial books – Marx in social philosophy, Engels in description of contemporary

7

industrial life. Both of them, and particularly Marx, were convinced that they had solved the riddles of man's existence. Marx never questioned, even in his time of total obscurity, that he was destined to be the intellectual master of the world, and Engels sustained him in this belief. Marx supposed that he had discovered the laws underlying human behaviour and that these laws would one day be accepted by the generality of mankind. Such convictions are no doubt held by the founder of every trivial sect. In Marx's case, they proved well-founded. At any rate nearly half the world acknowledges him as master, and it is essentially *The Communist Manifesto* which it acknowledges.

Intellectual self-confidence was common among nineteenth-century thinkers, and it has always been the mark of philosophers except the English variety: most of them pursue the Philosopher's Stone in some form of universal wisdom. Self-confidence was particularly strong in Hegel and his followers who dominated German philosophy when Marx entered on his academic studies at the universities of Bonn and Berlin. Hegel himself had been dead for some years; his spirit still walked the lecture rooms, and Marx learnt from it. Like other philosophers, Hegel sought for a world-system and claimed to have done better than his predecessors. They had been baffled by the problem that the world would not stand still. No sooner did they devise a universal system than the world changed into something else. Hegel made change itself the heart of his system. Moreover he laid down how change came about. A principle or idea – the thesis – was challenged by its opposite – the antithesis. From their conflict there emerged not the victory of one side or the other, but a combination of the two – the synthesis. In time this new thesis was again challenged by a new antithesis. A new synthesis emerged, and thus mankind rolled forward and upward. This was the Hegelian process of the dialectic.

Hegelian philosophy was a stroke of enlightenment. For the first time, thinkers made their peace with movement instead of insisting on a static universe. They were in fact fumbling towards the idea of evolution, which was perhaps the greatest creative idea of the nineteenth century. But Hegel could not tolerate the conception that things grew and changed of themselves. He still wanted to discover some outside force which drove them on and imagined that he had found it in the dialectic. To a sceptical English eye, the dialectic seems an arbitrary and unnatural form which breaks down at the first hurdle. After all, the conflict between male and female – thesis and antithesis – is also cooperation, though Hegel as a German did not perhaps like to admit it. Moreover this conflict does not produce a synthesis in the shape of a hermaphrodite, but a new being who is either male or female. However these are mundane objections. Marx's revision of Hegel had a different nature. The conflict which Hegel postulated was between ideas. Marx found the conflict in the world itself, and the ideas sprang from the conflict instead of causing it. In his own words, he found Hegelianism standing on its head and put it right way up. He called the result dialectical materialism.

In another aspect Marx did not quarrel with Hegel. Though Hegel had accepted movement and change, he was philosopher enough to jib at the thought that these would go on for ever. One day the dialectical process would reach its term. The ideal would be achieved. As a young man, Hegel thought that this ideal had been achieved with Napoleon. Later he was shrewd enough to abandon this illusion and discovered the ideal in the Prussian state, which had arrived at the perfect society. In this ingenious way, Hegelianism, which was based on change, became a doctrine of conservatism, with the dialectic reduced to a historic curiosity. Marx was a radical before he began as a philosopher, and a radical he remained. He certainly did not regard the Prussian state as ideal. But he, too, assumed that the dialectic would achieve its goal one day or another. The social conflicts which were the basis of his system would finally produce a synthesis where no conflicts were left, and history would come to an end. This synthesis was socialism, an ideal society or Utopia where everyone would be happy without conflict for ever more. The idea of a socialist Utopia was by no means new. Indeed dreamers had been describing it for many years. The novelty which Marx provided, according

9

to his own account, was to show how the ideal future would grow out of the practical present. There was no need to postulate some impossible change of heart. Dialectical materialism would compel men to live in Utopia whatever the promptings of their hearts.

Marx called this demonstration 'scientific'. His socialism sprang from an analysis of social forces, not from an abstract statement of wishes. Of course Marx wanted socialism to win and rigged the dialectic in order to ensure that it should. That is the way of philosophers. His theory was also implicitly a judgement in psychology. It assumed that men would behave as the social forces determined they should. The rich and powerful would always behave like the rich and powerful; the poor would always behave like the poor; ultimately the inhabitants of Utopia would always behave in a Utopian way. There was something odd in this when one reflects that Marx, the radical, came from a settled, respectable family and ought, by his own rule, to have been a conservative. This oddity was almost universal among later Marxists, most of whom, while preaching socialism, belonged to the class which socialism would destroy. It seems that the rules which philosophers lay down do not apply to philosophers themselves.

Marx was in tune with contemporary thought when he called his universal dogmas 'scientific'. Most scientists then imagined that they were approaching ever nearer to certainty and would ultimately formulate laws of universal validity. But even then they tried to observe first and to deduce laws from their observations. Marx, like Hegel before him, generalized about society before he studied it, and his later observations, though extremely laborious, were fitted into a system which already existed, a system moreover which was treated as complete once and for all. Marx never made a discovery in the scientific sense. He never had an illumination which turned his previous ideas upside down. He decided beforehand what he wanted to discover and then sure enough discovered it. In practice Marx and still more his friend Engels made many unavowed adjustments to their system, until by the end of their lives hardly any of it remained. At any rate it could be turned to almost any purpose from the most moderate to the most revolutionary. Despite this, Marx remained assertive and self-confident. He had somehow proved that socialism must come about, in the way that Newton – another authority now somewhat shaken – had proved the movements of the heavens.

As a student of society, Marx claimed to be an historian also, and his historical researches were great. Here too he was very much a man of his time. Nearly all nineteenth-century historians believed in Progress. They saw man's story as a record of almost uninterrupted improvement and were convinced that the Higher triumphed at each stage. Whatever happened next was right, a comforting doctrine for the victors. Yet Marx lacked the historical spirit even by nineteenth-century standards and still more by ours. The historian assembles data and is even more aware than the physical scientist how inadequate his data are. Much of the evidence on which we could base our knowledge of the past either has been destroyed or was never recorded. We guess from the few remaining fragments much as a geologist reconstructs a prehistoric monster from a single bone. Even at the present time, when thousands of trained experts are engaged in assembling and analysing the statistics of economic life, experts and governments have only the vaguest idea what has happened and no firm idea of what is likely to happen. There is little chance therefore of our reaching any very solid conclusions about early times when no reliable figures existed and there is not much information of any other kind. The only safe generalization we can make about man's record was propounded by Anatole France: 'He was born. He suffered. He died.' History is the great school of scepticism.

Marx operated before the historical outlook had been established. Those who studied history, and there were great names among them, had always sought to reduce the past to a system. Usually they treated the past as though it were the present happening at some different time. In Marx's lifetime, true history was beginning. He was not interested in it. It offered scepticism where he wanted certainty. It destroyed the foundations of all systems, when he had perfected the final system. Moreover, most practitioners of history were politically conservative, and this, too, set Marx against them. Study of the past often turns into love of the past and a desire to keep it. In *The Communist Manifesto* and elsewhere, Marx pointed to this occupational disease of historians. All the same, it was a misfortune that Marx matured before the historical idea had reshaped men's habits of thought. He was to show himself later a historical researcher of the first order, and a truly historical approach might have freed him from the rigid frame of dialectical materialism.

Marx once described his system as an amalgamation of German philosophy, French politics, and English economics. When he finished his university studies, he was secure only in his philosophy. He had discovered, as he supposed, the pattern of historical change. He did not know its practical expression or its driving force. These discoveries were more or less forced on him by the accidents of life. He spent a year or two in Cologne as a radical journalist – the only time when he earned his own living. After this he depended on remittances from Engels and no doubt murmured: 'Capital! Capital!' as each instalment arrived. His journalism was too radical for the Prussian authorities, and he became a political exile in Paris. Here he discovered the practical expression of the dialectic soon enough. It was revolution, the clash, in Hegelian terms, between thesis and antithesis. Though half a century had passed since the great revolution, all French political life centred on it. Nearly everyone agreed that the revolution had made a fundamental change in French affairs. Before it there had been the *ancien régime* of feudalism. After it, there was the new order of bourgeois society. Divine right had been replaced by the rights of man. Reason had taken the place of tradition. The change had been rapid. Five years, between 1789 and 1794, had been enough to wipe out the legacy of many centuries and to give France an entirely new appearance.

Historians have chipped away some parts of this picture. Only a few years later Tocqueville, for instance, was to show that much of the new revolutionary society had been growing in the old one and had been shaped by what went before.

Nevertheless, the French revolution had been truly revolutionary. Nearly all the modern world stems from it, even though the debt is now less acknowledged. It was not surprising that men expected new revolutions in France as the only possible form of change and that they expected to see similar revolutions in other European countries. Frenchmen were divided only into those who were preparing to resist the next revolution and those who were working or hoping for it. Marx at once accepted from the French radicals with whom he associated the belief that revolution was waiting at the door.

Marx also accepted their view that the revolution would be short and sharp. Blanqui, the most famous French revolutionary, expressed this in the words: 'It takes twenty-four hours to make a revolution.' The great French revolution seemed to teach this lesson. It had been punctuated by 'days', each of which had an immediate political effect. The fall of the Bastille on 14 July 1789 had ended the absolute monarchy; 10 August 1792 had ended constitutional monarchy; 9 Thermidor had ended the revolution. New revolutions would happen in the same way. The radicals would seize power at a single stroke, and the revolution would be accomplished.

Frenchmen had probed deeply into an analysis of who stood on the opposing sides of the barricades. This analysis was class in its crudest form. The original revolution had been made against the territorial or feudal aristocracy by the bourgeoisie – in English, less precisely, the middle class. The Jacobin revolution had been made against the bourgeoisie by the people, the poor, or the masses. This revolution, which had been defeated, would be repeated more successfully in the near future. The analysis had by now become more refined. The Jacobins were dismissed as petit bourgeois – the shopkeepers and small tradesmen, not the real people. The poor had acquired a new, more romantic description. They were the proletariat – those who had no property except their labour and their children. They alone would make a revolution without reserves.

Later generations often saw Marx as the special advocate of class warfare or even as its inventor. In fact, Marx as a class-warrior was merely repeating the accepted commonplace of his time. Every writer described society in class terms, as witness Disraeli's famous reference to the Two Nations. Every politician interpreted events on a class basis and calculated actions with an eye to their class results. In England, the Reform Bill of 1832 was regarded as a victory of the middle classes over the privileged aristocracy, and the repeal of the Corn Laws, still more precisely, as a victory of the industrial capitalists over the landowners. In France everything which followed from the revolution of 1830 was known as bourgeois, up to Louis Philippe who gloried in the title of the bourgeois king. In 1830 Laffitte, a leading banker, exclaimed correctly: 'Now the bankers will rule.' Every constitutional country had a limited franchise, elaborately devised to ensure that the middle classes were included and the masses left out. It was tempting to conclude from this that, since the bourgeoisie appeared to have become rich by acquiring political power, the proletariat could also escape from their misery by a further revolution of their own.

It was also tempting to conclude that political power sprang from the franchise and that therefore the proletariat would gain political power once they had the vote. Universal suffrage was the more or less universal aim of revolutionaries before 1848. The Chartists in England, who were regarded at any rate by Marx as class-conscious proletarians, made universal suffrage the key point of the People's Charter. The Chartist leaders, and still more no doubt their followers, had no clear idea what practical acts a People's Parliament would perform. The acquisition of power was all that mattered. The benefits would then follow of themselves.

These somewhat crude views did not really accord with the dialectical system which Marx had already formulated. Though he might speak of revolution as the midwife of historical change, he knew that such change took much longer than Blanqui's twenty-four hours. Indeed the dialectic made more sense as an evolutionary doctrine than as a call to revolution. If the bourgeoisie had taken centuries to mature, the proletariat would take centuries more. Again, Marx thought in terms of society, not of the state, and regarded the state simply as the political expression of the social system. Blanqui and his like thought that all would be well if they sat in the Ministry of the Interior, whether voted there or not, and appointed radicals as prefects. Marx was concerned to change society or rather, if he adhered rigidly to his system, expected society to change in the way that he wanted. Harold Laski remarked, some twenty years ago, that the Labour government of 1945, which was put in power by popular vote and did what the people wanted, was nearer the Marxist idea than any of the governments thrown up by revolution, French, Russian or other.

It is also possible to criticize the French revolutionary view of history by greater knowledge of history itself. The economic encroachments of the French bourgeoisie on the aristocracy, for instance, may have helped to produce the political revolution. But later political events did not much affect the further economic advance of the bourgeoisie, which went on regardless of the particular political system. Nor is it true that changes were determined solely by class allegiances. The English Reform Bill was carried by a parliament of landlords, and the Corn Laws were repealed by a parliament in which there were not more than half a dozen industrial capitalists. Nor were the Chartist leaders for the most part members of the working class. They were lawyers, journalists, and professional agitators; Feargus O'Connor, the most oratorically violent of them, was a landowner. Experience was also to show that men do not always vote for others of their own class or according to their class interest, when they get the vote. The British middle classes continued to vote for landowners, and the British workers later on were to vote for members of the middle class, so much so that by the later twentieth century even the Labour party was hard pressed to find working-class candidates.

Marx knew that the vote did not of itself determine political power. But he believed that property did. This was characteristic of a legally-trained mind in a legal, orderly age. Of course property determines power, so long as the rights of property are respected. But there are times when power comes first. The Norman barons in England, for instance, were not powerful because they owned feudal property. They owned property because they were powerful or, in more brutal terms, because they had conquered the country. Later in the nineteenth century, Europeans acquired property all over the continent of Africa, and this seemed to make them powerful. They dressed this up with all kinds of legal pretences, but the true basis of their power was expressed by Hilaire Belloc in the words:

> We have the Maxim gun,
> And they have not.

Marx was to condemn the professors who ran the German revolution of 1848 for their obsession with legal forms. But he had the same obsession in a more covert way. He tended to suppose that title-deeds had some value or authority in themselves, much as the French peasants of 1789 thought that they would be free if they burnt the documents in the neighbouring castle.

This is only to say that Marx was a man of his time, shackled, despite his originality, to its conventions. When he thought in a detached way, he recognized that social change was a slow process, little affected by political events. But, as a restless polemical revolutionary, he rarely thought in a detached way. He was told in Paris correctly that a new revolution was coming and, less correctly, that it would inaugurate the last stage of historical change. He took this as good news. It was impossible for him to resist the promise that Utopia was just round the corner. With pardonable inconsistency, he inserted Blanqui into his system and then left Hegel and Blanqui to fight things out.

Marx was dissatisfied with his system for a different reason. He had found a pattern of conflict in the dialectic. He had found the conflicting parties in the bourgeoisie and the proletariat. He had not found a driving force for the conflict between them. Unless he did so, he would have to postulate some Ideal, even if it were only the Ideal of revolution, as the driving force, and would thus be back, despite all his hardheaded contempt, at Hegelian idealism. Where was the built-in force, not in men's minds, which drove them into social action?

The answer was not far to seek in a materialist age. The answer was the pursuit of wealth, an answer given by the writers of political economy. The answer had been obscured in France by the political turmoils of revolution. It was given with one accord by all thinkers in England. Once more accident opened the door of revelation to Marx. Exile from Germany had led him to discover the revolutionary politics of the dialectic in France. Now a private friendship led Marx to discover the economic basis for revolution in England.

The friend was Engels, the only lasting friend whom Marx ever had. Friedrich Engels was two years younger than Marx. He, too, was an eager radical, but academically less equipped. His only academic experience was to have attended a few university lectures at Berlin during his year of military service. Otherwise he was self-educated, always ready to get up a new subject and shape it, without much knowledge, into a systematic simple form. Unlike most revolutionaries, Engels earned his living. His father was a cotton merchant, and Engels spent much of his life conducting the Manchester office of the family firm. He became a reasonably wealthy man. He was a respected figure in Manchester society; hunted two days a week with the Cheshire – valuable training, he contended, for a future commander of revolutionary armies; and was able later both to keep Marx in moderate comfort and himself to retire prosperously at the age of fifty. Wealth did not shake his revolutionary views. He lived with an Irish factory girl, Mary Burns, and, when she died, with her sister Lizzie, whom he finally married. Where Marx still breathed the rather stale air of the French revolution, Engels experienced something fresher: the industrial revolution which had covered Lancashire with cotton mills. Here was class war in plain economic terms, and Engels's first work described the Condition of the English Working Class in 1844. It is still a historical authority of the first importance, even though apologists for capitalism have criticized its exaggerations.

In 1844 Engels met Marx in Paris and established a friendship which was never shaken. Marx provided philosophical grasp and ruthless domination over others; Engels provided experience and of course money. When Engels described conditions in Lancashire and subsequently took Marx on a visit there, Marx realized that he had found the key to historic change. The driving force was not in men's minds, but in the system of production. The capitalists of industrial Lancashire were not being peculiarly wicked when they forced men and women to work for long hours and low wages. They were merely acting according to their economic needs. Similarly the Lancashire workers were not being peculiarly altruistic when they joined together in trade unions or cooperatives. They too were responding to the economic pressures on them.

Lancashire seemed to display the workings of the dialectic in its simplest form. The capitalists had proceeded from small factories to large ones. The lesser capitalists had been squeezed out by the greater. The workers had lost what little property they possessed, as notably the power looms had destroyed the handloom-weavers with their home industry. Soon the entire population of Lancashire would be crowded into the stifling mills. A few capitalists would engross all the power and wealth. The factory workers would unite, as they were already doing in the Chartist movement. They would take over the factories, and with this private property would come to an end. Marx did not yet understand the theoretical reasons for these developments. This was to come only when he studied the English economists during the long years of his exile in London after the failure of the 1848 revolutions. But he at once made the essential economic generalization. Just as all the world – or at least all Europe, which for Marx amounted to much the same thing – would follow politically the pattern of the French revolution, so economically it would follow the pattern of industrial Lancashire. Though Marx was a materialist only in a philosophic sense, it no doubt gave him pleasure that the coming revolution, though political in appearance, would have an economic cause.

Once more Marx had made a universal generalization from a single example. For him, the cotton industry was synonymous with capitalism, and he supposed that all other industries would follow its rules. He thought also that he and Engels were living in an age of fully-developed capitalism, when in fact capitalism had hardly started. There was really very little modern about the textile industry, which was no more than the application of steam-power to an industry which had existed for centuries. The cotton industry flourishes only in backward countries with a predominantly agrarian population, as later experience has shown. Industrial England of 1847, though very impressive to contemporaries, now appears crude and backward, not much higher than, say, the present level of India. The true industrial revolution began only with the railways, which in their turn launched the age of iron and steel. This, too, has given way to the age of the internal combustion-engine and electronics. Marx thought too narrowly in economic terms of capital and failed to allow for the endlessly stimulating effect of human invention. When one industry was overloaded with capital, new channels were soon opened elsewhere.

On the other side, Marx, prompted by Engels, equated the workers in the cotton mills with the proletariat. This was a false equation. The proletariat, if the phrase meant anything, were at the very bottom of the social ladder and possessed literally nothing. They were driven to revolt by their increasing misery. The industrial workers had a higher standard of life than most members of the lower classes even in 1844, when Engels studied them, and their standard of life moved steadily upwards. Even in Marx's time, they had a form of property in the cooperative stores, and soon they acquired their own houses. Latter-day capitalism is often impeded by the fact that workers are too rooted in their possessions to be willing to move into new industries elsewhere. The trade union leaders whom Marx met later dressed like respectable bourgeois, with gold watch-chains across their stomachs.

Already, factory workers were not the stuff of which rioters were made. They were no longer Luddites. Still less did they man the barricades. Their chosen weapon of conflict was the strike, and the object of a strike was to reach agreement with the employer, of course on favourable terms, not to get rid of him. Marx did not grasp this, and later Communists followed his

19

teaching. For them every settlement of a strike was 'treachery' by the union leaders. Marx and his followers supposed that one day the strike would become an aggressive weapon, designed to take over the factories. This was to misunderstand its essential nature as a method of bargaining. Without the boss, no bargaining would be possible. Still, Marx was stuck with his equation. Henceforth the industrial workers were his proletariat. The true proletariat were dismissed as down-and-outs, *Lumpenproletariat* in Marx's term. They were good-for-nothings and, though they were the only people to provide riots, Marx was not surprised when these riots proved of no purpose.

Marx's system was now complete in skeleton form: dialectical pattern, political revolutionary outcome, economic driving force. He still had to announce his system to the world and, like any religious teacher, he needed disciples. He found them among Germans living in Paris, Brussels, and London. Some of them were political refugees; some had moved in order to practise their trade. None of them was a proletarian in the new Marxist sense; none, that is, was a factory worker. Their occupations provide striking examples of the class from whom revolutionaries are often drawn. Most of them were tailors – an occupation which gives a man much time for solitary revolutionary reflection and also perhaps an intimate distaste for the upper classes. Then came a type-setter, a cobbler, a watchmaker, a painter of miniatures, a few students, a Prussian officer who had been cashiered, and Marx's aristocratic brother-in-law. Engels no doubt had a bigger income than that of all the other German revolutionaries put together.

There was nothing surprising in their unproletarian character. On the contrary, all experience shows that revolutionaries come from those who are economically independent, not from factory workers. Very few revolutionary leaders have done manual work, and those who did soon abandoned it for political activities. The factory worker wants higher wages and better conditions, not a revolution. It is the man on his own who wants to remake society, and moreover he can happily defy those in power without economic risk. In old England the village cobbler was always the radical and the Dissenter. After all, the lord of the manor had to have his boots made and mended, whatever the cobbler's political opinions. The independent craftsman, like the intellectual, cannot be dismissed from his job. His skill protects him from the penalties which society imposes on the nonconformist. Marx's original disciples were the stuff from which all later Communists were made.

The story of their organizations was a complicated tangle, significant only to themselves. The various high-sounding bodies probably never had more than half a dozen members each. This is no reproach. Twelve men were enough to start off Christianity. The original body was a secret society in Paris, called characteristically the League of the Just. This was vaguely associated with the conspiratorial societies run by Blanqui and is supposed to have taken some part in his attempt at revolution in 1839. This was little more than a riot in a café, and the Just cannot have done much. However three of them removed to London, where they constituted the German Workers' Educational League. Engels attended a meeting and in 1845 introduced Marx. Marx approved of their method: study, not conspiracy. He had now been turned out of Paris and had settled in Brussels. There he set up a similar organization, the German Working Men's Association. Engels, to whom Paris was not barred, tried not very successfully to start something of the kind there also.

On top of these more or less imaginary bodies Marx then constructed a federation, which he called the Communist Correspondence Committee. Soon afterwards it changed its name to the Communist League. By 1847 Marx decided that it was time for the League to meet. A delegate conference was summoned to London in November. Shortly before it met the London branch brought out a single number of an organ entitled *The Communist Journal*. It was not memorable except for the fact that it bore on its masthead the words: 'Proletarians of all lands, unite!' The delegates turned out to be a hundred or so, their ranks swelled by curious English Chartists, who had come to demonstrate their sympathy with Poland.

Marx attended in person. He listened impatiently while the worthy tailors lamented the wickedness of capitalism and preached universal brotherhood. He rose and denounced brotherhood in the name of the class war. The tailors were entranced. Where they relied on sentiment, a learned man explained to them how society worked and placed the key to the future in their hands. They invited Marx to write a declaration of principles for them. He agreed.

Marx returned to Brussels. He took with him an emotional declaration about socialism by two members of the London group, the solitary issue of *The Communist Journal,* and a catechism on the Principles of Communism which Engels had drafted in the train from Manchester to London. As well, Marx had his own library in Brussels. Later Engels sent a few more ideas by letter, particularly the suggestion that the declaration should be called a Manifesto. Marx took a good deal from the catechism. He accepted for instance the twist which Engels had given to the meaning of 'proletarian':

The proletariat is the working class of the nineteenth century....
It was created by the industrial revolution which took place in England during the second half of the eighteenth century and which has repeated itself in all the civilized countries of the world.

Marx accepted also the doctrine laid down by Engels that capitalism would produce crises of over-production, as indeed it had done in 1847, and that the abolition of private property would be the inevitable outcome. Marx reproduced, sometimes almost word for word, some passages from *The Poverty of Philosophy,* a book he had written attacking Proudhon, and some from *The German Ideology,* a joint production with Engels which was not published in their lifetime. Despite these borrowings, the *Manifesto* had a character all its own. It is usual to consider it as the joint work of Marx and Engels. In fact, as Engels repeatedly insisted, the actual composition was the work of Marx alone, and his readiness to put Engels's name also on the title page was a remarkable example of intellectual generosity.

In arrangement, the *Manifesto* followed the catechism pretty closely. Sections 1 and 2 correspond to questions-and-answers 1 to 23. Section 3 expands question-and-answer 24. Section 4 corresponds to question-and-answer 25. This last section is a hasty botched affair, and it looks as though Marx had to wind up in a hurry. We know this to be the case. On 26 January 1848 the London committee sent an ultimatum to Brussels. Citizen Marx was warned that, unless he produced his Manifesto by 1 February, 'further measures will have to be taken against him'. Marx just made his deadline. The Londoners did not venture to make any corrections to the Manifesto which had been drafted in their name. They handed the manuscript to a German printer in Bishopsgate, who published it as a pamphlet of twenty-three pages before the end of February. This first edition contained a number of proof-reading errors. A corrected edition was brought out some time in April or May, and this edition, which was reproduced unchanged in 1866, is the basis for all later editions of the German text, itself the original for all translations.

The Communist League played no further part in history. Some of its members returned to Germany after the revolutions of March 1848 and engaged in radical activities. Marx himself ran a radical newspaper in the Rhineland. Engels, the military expert, was an officer in the short-lived radical uprising in Baden. Afterwards they all returned to England as political exiles. In 1852 the Communist League was formally dissolved. It had done its good deed for mankind when it prompted Karl Marx to write *The Communist Manifesto*.

Marx was not only a considerable thinker. He was also, when he wanted to be, a brilliant and direct writer. An early friend, Moses Hess, described him as 'the greatest, perhaps *the one genuine philosopher* now alive', and added: 'Imagine Rousseau, Voltaire, Holbach, Lessing, Heine, and Hegel united in one person – I say united, not lumped together – and you have Dr Marx.' Usually Marx did not want to be direct or simple. His previous works had been ponderously phrased with elaborate twists of the dialectic. At the other extreme, he had a weakness for personal abuse – funny enough, but levelled against individuals now usually forgotten. The *Manifesto* was exposition in simple style, designed no doubt for the simple tailors of the Communist League. Nevertheless it contains a full exposition of Marx's system, so far as he had developed it. Curiously, it is the only straightforward exposition in the Marxist canon. His later ones are either asides in his larger works or else carefully dressed in moderate form to suit the narrow-minded outlook of English trade unionists. In the *Manifesto* Marx did not have to trim his views for the sake of his audience and, on the whole, did not run after personal feuds, though even here he could not resist some jibes at his rivals.

The *Manifesto* was not of course a detached work of political philosophy, elaborated in the calm of a scholar's study. It was written in haste for a particular group of people – German craftsmen in exile – and for a particular occasion – the eve of the 1848 revolutions. It is not uncommon for observers to foretell a revolution, though they are by no means always right, and no revolutions have been more generally foretold than those which swept most of the European continent in 1848. Not only revolutionaries foretold them. Leading Conservatives agreed. Metternich announced that he was sustaining 'a rotten edifice'. King Frederick William IV of Prussia summoned Herwegh, the revolutionary poet, in order to salute 'a worthy opponent' and the man of the future. Most observers also agreed with Marx that the revolutions would have a social or economic cause. And so they had, though not the cause which Marx propounded. He attributed the coming revolutions to capitalism. It would be truer to say that they were caused by lack of capitalism. Apart from Russia, which had hardly begun to share European developments, two countries paradoxically escaped serious revolutionary disturbance. They were Great Britain and Belgium, the two countries in which industrialization was most advanced.

The fundamental cause of the 1848 revolutions was the increase in population which had become general since the beginning of the century. Historians do not agree why this increase took place. Perhaps it was due to improved medical services; perhaps to cultivation of the humdrum potato. At any rate, the inhabitants of the countryside crowded into the towns, and there found few factories to employ them. Revolutions occurred in almost every European city with more than 50,000 inhabitants. The occasion for the revolutions was hunger: failure of the potato crop in 1846 and subsequent years, failure of the wheat harvest in 1847. Soup kitchens were the prelude to revolution. The revolutionaries might talk about socialism. Those who actually revolted wanted 'the right to work' – more capitalism, not its abolition.

The proletariat was not the only revolutionary class in 1848, either in the traditional or in the Marxist sense, whatever Marx himself might say. Intellectual elements of the bourgeoisie were also revolutionary, though not according to Marx's programme. In France they wanted universal suffrage and the republic. In central Europe they wanted constitutional systems, in other words the completion and extension of the French revolution. They also wanted national unity in some form or another, first in Germany and Italy, and then, to most people's surprise or disapproval – including most strongly the disapproval of Marx and Engels – in the forgotten lands of eastern Europe. The Slavs and other peoples without a history announced their rebirth. Nationalism was a stronger force than economics in most of the revolutions of 1848. The champions of national unification were the heroes in 1848. Afterwards in the years of exile the figures with the greatest prestige were Mazzini, the prophet of Italian nationalism, and Kossuth, Governor of independent Hungary. Dr Marx was much annoyed.

Marx himself dismissed the peasants as a reactionary force without revolutionary significance. Other revolutionaries did much the same. The revolution passed from one town to the next by train and telegraph, just as the revolutionaries themselves passed by train through an ignored countryside. Nevertheless the revolutions were serious only when the peasants were drawn into them. The French revolution remained a purely urban affair and was therefore easily snuffed out once the peasants were mobilized against it. In central Europe the peasants wanted to shake off the *robot* or labour-rent and to achieve freedom of movement. This put them on the revolutionary side until their demands were fulfilled. Then they too swung over to conservatism, and the revolutions were defeated.

The experience of the 1848 revolutions did not conform to the Marxist pattern. The initial outbreaks usually came from the down-and-outs or *Lumpenproletariat*, a most undesirable class from the Marxist point of view. The peasants alone made revolution really dangerous, again a breach of Marxist rules. Bourgeois intellectuals kept things going, and their enthusiasm was far more for nationalism than for social reform. No professional revolutionary managed to be on hand when a revolution started, and few of them played a significant part afterwards. Though they had preached universal suffrage, none of them succeeded at the polls, even to the extent of being elected to a parish council. Blanqui indeed proposed that elections should be put off until the people had received an education in democratic principles and, when asked how long this postponement would last, replied: 'Perhaps for months, perhaps for years.' Proudhon, also a revolutionary of sorts and according to Marx a stupid one, propounded the disturbing law: 'Universal suffrage is counter-revolution.' Though stupid, Proudhon turned out to be right.

Of course social questions counted for much during the period of revolution. Revolutions always disturb settled relations in class as in everything else. The religious revolutions of the sixteenth and seventeenth centuries had a most unsettling social effect, which some historians indeed treat as their underlying cause. It is not surprising that social upheaval was still greater in 1848, when revolutionary ideas had taken a clear social form. But it was mainly upheaval, not the construction of a new society. A friend of Tocqueville's heard his man servant say: 'Next Sunday *we* shall be eating the wing of the chicken,' and the maid replied: 'Next Sunday *we* shall be wearing the fine clothes.' When Sunday came, they duly waited at table. Tocqueville himself feared one night that his houseporter intended to assassinate him and kept a firm grip on his pistol. But he rang the doorbell without fear the next night.

26

The industrial workers took little part in the revolution. Even in Great Britain there were demonstrations in London and Glasgow, but not in industrial Lancashire. Though the social question was posed, socialism was not aired as a practical programme.

Marx would have regarded these mundane objections as irrelevant. Essentially he was a prophet, not a philosopher. He invoked history only when it was going his way and, if events did not fit in with his system, so much the worse for events. This has been called the unity of theory and action. In Marx's own words: 'Philosophers have only given different *interpretations* of the world; the important thing is to make it different.' His test of a system was not so much whether it corresponded to reality as whether it would help to stimulate the changes which he wanted. The Marxist system was a propagandist myth, deceptively adorned with scientific analysis. Every word and argument of *The Communist Manifesto* was designed to produce an effect. This was true even of the title. The document purported to be the manifesto of the Communist Party. No such party existed at that time, and one object of the manifesto was to call it into existence. Nor had 'Communists of various nationalities assembled in London and sketched the following manifesto', as stated on the first page. It had been written by Marx alone. The one incontrovertible sentence in the manifesto was the first, the famous sentence which announced: 'A spectre is haunting Europe – the spectre of Communism'. Communism was indeed a spectre, a ghost, with which reactionaries gave themselves a fright and concealed their own incompetence. This remains true. Anti-Communism causes more trouble in the world than ever Communism does or did. However Marx hardly meant his sentence to be taken in this sense.

Why *Communist*? As Engels explained in his 1888 preface, socialism was not then a fighting word. It was used for all kinds of Utopian schemes devised by non-proletarian writers. Communist was both older and more defiantly revolutionary. It meant rigorously the community of goods and therewith the total abolition of private property. It harked back to the legendary state of primitive communism which, according to Engels, had existed before the economic Fall. Communism had been haunting the world as a spectre long before the days of Marx and Engels. It was an accusation levelled against the early Christians and against the Anabaptists of the sixteenth century. Agrarian Communism was a dreaded prospect during the French revolution and sent even Jacobins scuttling under the protection of Napoleon. The word also evoked the Commune of Paris, which had been the most advanced revolutionary force in 1793. The two words had of course little real association, Commune being merely a French term for municipal government. But the link served to give the bourgeoisie a fright, and thus to satisfy Marx's sense of humour.

All this was preliminary to the real argument or rather to the series of dogmas with their deceptive air of obvious truth. The first was also the most decisive: 'The history of all hitherto existing societies is the history of class struggles.' This sounds simple, but is it true? Sometimes there have been class struggles, though more rarely than Marx made out. Often there has been class cooperation, as for instance against foreign enemies. More often still men have gone on with their work and not thought about the class struggle one way or the other. Marx was really saying that history ought to have been the history of class struggles. But history failed to obey Marx's instruction. For most of the time most men did not want to overthrow their superiors or even to climb into their ranks. This was no doubt tiresome for Marx and other revolutionaries. But that is how it was, and Marx would have saved his followers much trouble if he had recognized that class struggle is something men go in for only when they have to.

Marx provided a different explanation. Earlier class struggles had not been decisive because there were so many classes. Marx had a simple pattern of history: feudalism, capitalism, socialism. Sometimes, when he remembered the classical world, he threw in also the ancient or, as he called it, the Asiatic system of production. But for practical purposes he stuck to the way in which capitalism had succeeded feudalism. He insisted that by 1847, his time of writing, the triumph of capitalism was complete. The bourgeoisie had established 'exclusive political sway' and the state had become 'but a committee for managing the common affairs of the whole bourgeoisie'. This was another *ought* statement. Maybe it ought to have happened, but it had not except perhaps in France. Landowners still predominated in the British political system, and monarchs far from bourgeois ruled most of Europe until the twentieth century. Moreover the state did not conduct affairs exclusively in either feudal or bourgeois interests. The state had a life of its own and was sustained by monarchs or administrators, who thought in terms of its interests. Perhaps the greatest blindness in Marx's system was the refusal to recognize the independent managers in both political and economic affairs. The British parliament had just passed the Ten Hours Act, limiting the hours of work in factories, as a measure of social benefit, and Bismarck later was to inaugurate social welfare in Germany, simply from a calculation that this would strengthen the independence of his state against all classes, bourgeois even more than proletarian.

The bourgeoisie, according to Marx, were not content to establish their domination in a single country. They imposed Free Trade throughout the world. Here again Marx was saying what ought to happen by his rules or what the bourgeoisie ought to do if they understood economics as well as he did. But Free Trade also did not happen, or only for a short time. States protected their separate existences by tariffs, so much so that in the twentieth century capitalism enormously reinforced national independence instead of destroying it. However the bourgeoisie were due to run into trouble of their own making. There would be an epidemic 'that, in all earlier epochs, would have seemed an absurdity – the epidemic of over-production'. This was the economic analysis which Marx had learnt from Engels and which partly corresponded with reality so far as the great crisis of 1847 was concerned. As yet, Marx had no theoretical explanation why these crises of over-production occurred, other than the innate wickedness of the capitalists in driving the workers down to a starvation level. Later, after many years of research, Marx thought that he had discovered the economic laws which compelled capitalists to be wicked whether they wanted to be or not. But recurring and ever sharper crises were an assumption of his system before he found the reasons for them.

Crises were only one side of the Marxist system. The other, equally essential point was that, in Marx's words, the bourgeoisie produced their own grave-diggers. These were of course the proletariat or, in his alternative definition, the industrial working class. As the result of the industrial revolution, the workers lost their few scraps of property and were herded together in large towns. They were compelled to combine in order to resist the constant lowering of their wages. Marx foretold that they would pass over to the offensive and would be driven to destroy the entire system of private property. Previously class rule had been the rule of a minority. The proletariat were 'the immense majority'. Therefore their rule would be conducted in the interests of everyone. Class rule, in the old sense, would come to an end. The final Hegelian synthesis would be achieved.

Sometimes Marx implied that the proletariat would include everyone except the few remaining capitalists. Sometimes he recognized that other classes would continue to litter the historical stage. His judgement of them was almost uniformly hostile. The lower middle class – shopkeepers, artisans, and peasants – would fight to save their own existence. 'They are therefore not revolutionary, but conservative. Nay more, they are reactionary, for they try to roll back the wheel of history.' In other words they disagreed with Marx. The social scum or *Lumpenproletariat* were even worse. Though they might initially be 'swept into the movement by a proletarian revolution', they were more likely to become 'a bribed tool of reactionary intrigue'. One class curiously escapes Marx's general condemnation. Some bourgeois ideologists 'have raised themselves to the level of comprehending theoretically the historical movement as a whole'. They therefore 'cut themselves adrift and join the revolutionary class, the class that holds the future in its hands'. It is not difficult to guess the enlightened bourgeois individuals who had thus defied the rigour of Marxist rules.

They were none other than Marx and, as a generous concession, Engels.

The first section of the *Manifesto,* here concluded, explains how society had developed and how it would develop. It was analysis, not a call to action, and might well tempt a bourgeois ideologist to wait for the inevitable rising of the proletariat. The second section is of a more practical nature. It is devoted to the Communists, who they are and what they should do. The definition of Communists is simple: they were the ones who understood what was happening in the world, a definition which again limited them to Marx and Engels. The Communists had 'no interests separate and apart from those of the proletariat as a whole' – a commendation which assumed that the proletariat would agree to have only the interests which Marx said it ought to have. The Communist programme was the abolition of private property or, to be more precise, the abolition of the private ownership of capital. Marx ran off the rails at this point. The thought of the bourgeoisie, upholding the sanctity of private property while it turned the vast majority into wage-slaves, stirred his invective, and he forgot that he was giving the Communists and proletariat practical guidance for political action. Probably he was now harassed by the impatience of the London committee and stuck in a denunciation of the bourgeoisie which really belonged to the first section.

The denunciation is very funny. It is reinforced by Marx's historical view that ideas and institutions spring from the society around them and do not have an independent existence. Many later historians have made their living and their reputation from this generalization. Marx is particularly enjoyable when he answers the accusation that Communists wished to abolish the family and to introduce community of women. The bourgeois, he remarks, regards his wife as an instrument of production; no wonder he expects her to be nationalized. In any case, the bourgeoisie already practice community of women. Not content with common prostitutes, 'they take the greatest pleasure in seducing each other's wives'.

The argument becomes more serious when Marx answers

the charge that Communists sought to abolish countries and nationality. Most revolutionaries at this time believed that national freedom and unification should be their most urgent aim, and nationalism was indeed to eclipse the social question during the revolutions of 1848. Marx prided himself on his internationalism and was as much at home with French revolutionaries or English Chartists as with German radicals, or so he thought. Besides, he wanted revolutionaries to concentrate on the class struggle. He therefore insists that only those who have a stake in a country – in the literal sense of owning property – can feel loyalty to it. The proletariat by definition have no property. Therefore they have no country. 'We cannot take from them what they have not got.' In any case, the spread of capitalism throughout the world was already destroying 'national differences and antagonisms between peoples', and the supremacy of the proletariat would cause them to vanish still faster. This was common Free Trade doctrine at the time, held by such bourgeois radicals as Bright and Cobden, whom usually Marx despised.

Marx had laid down at the outset that all struggles were class struggles. Clearly this must also apply to struggles between nations. Therefore 'in proportion as the antagonism between classes within the nation vanishes, the hostility of one nation to another will come to an end'. There is an assumption here, though of course not admitted by Marx, that the proletariat were more altruistic than other classes, an assumption not altogether borne out by later events. Undoubtedly some national conflicts sprang from what Marx called 'the exploitation of one nation by another'. This was true of the Irish struggle against the English and of the various Slav movements against the Germans. Marx duly sympathized with the Irish and urged the English workers to do the same. Later he came to believe that the English workers were corrupted into cooperating with their exploiters as long as they had the Irish to cooperate against, and he therefore held that the freeing of Ireland must be a preliminary to the victory of the proletariat in England. This was ingenious and even clearsighted. Marx's vision was less sure when it came to the Slavs. Engels at any rate held that their fate was to be absorbed into the superior culture of the German nation, and Marx did not openly disagree with him.

More than this, Marx's doctrine ignored the cases when national conflict sprang from the rivalry of more or less equal nations, each determined to be master. One proletariat might be tempted to challenge another, as later events have demonstrated. If capitalists could work against each other, surely proletarians might do the same. There was in Marx a curious idea that class conflicts occurred only between classes and never within them, an idea which ran counter to all economic experience. The truth is that Marx had no clear grasp of nationalism, only a desire to discredit the champions of national freedom, who were his revolutionary rivals. Marx's doctrine of proletarian freedom from national sentiment was the foundation-stone of the later Socialist Internationals, the First led by Marx himself. When challenged by national loyalties, these Internationals failed to hold their ground. The Second International perished with the first World war. The Third was dissolved during what the Russian Communists rightly called 'the Great Patriotic War'.

Marx reverts with a jerk to his immediate task of defining the Communist programme. The first step was for the proletariat to become the ruling class or, as Marx calls it, 'to win the battle of democracy'. The *Manifesto* itself does not contain Marx's famous phrase – 'the dictatorship of the proletariat'. But the idea is there, though the phrase is not. The proletariat would wrest all capital from the bourgeoisie and 'would centralize all instruments of production in the hands of the state'. This is in rather odd contrast with the principle laid down by Marx earlier in the *Manifesto* that economic change always preceded and caused political change. Here he is saying the opposite, and no wonder. Otherwise he would be trapped, as some later Marxists were, into waiting upon events. His escape from this danger was a logical contradiction, which he passed over by listing ten reforms which the victorious proletariat could at once undertake. Most of them have been carried by states far from proletarian. However Marx is now set for

33

Utopia. Once the proletariat rules, classes and class antagonisms will disappear. Then 'we shall have an association in which the free development of each is the condition for the free development of all'.

This concludes the serious argument of *The Communist Manifesto*. A few years later Marx summarized what he regarded as the new points in it. He wrote in 1852:

Long before me bourgeois historians had described the historical development of the class struggle in modern society, and bourgeois economists the anatomy of classes. What I did that was new was to prove (1) that the existence of classes is only bound up with *particular, historic phases in the development of production;* (2) that the class struggle necessarily leads *to the dictatorship of the proletariat;* (3) that this dictatorship itself only constitutes the transition to the *abolition of all classes* and to *classless society.*

This is a strange mixture of true and false. Marx had an odd conception of 'proof'. The tribute to his predecessors is fair and generous. Again, he had hit on a good idea, though an obvious one, when he showed that classes were shaped by changing social circumstances. But he could prove his second point, that the class struggle necessarily led to the dictatorship of the proletariat, only by relying on the dialectic. Since the bourgeoisie, being in conflict with the feudal aristocracy, had succeeded in establishing their dictatorship – in fact a questionable bit of history – it followed that the proletariat, now in conflict with the bourgeoisie, would do the same. The third point, that proletarian dictatorship would lead to a classless society, was not proved at all. It rested solely on the Hegelian belief that ultimately the dialectic process would come to an end. The Ideal would become the Real. Marx simply asserted that this would happen when the proletariat ruled.

There was more to come of *The Communist Manifesto*. Marx was never one to lay down his pen without an attack on his socialist rivals. There is a significant little point. In the preceding sections of the *Manifesto*, Marx sharpened and clarified the arguments which Engels had set down in his *Communist Catechism*, and the result was shorter as well as more effective. When Marx came to the rival socialists, he was both longer and more vituperative then Engels had been. The section is a curious period piece, though with some flashes of insight and more of misunderstanding. No one bothers any more about Young England or even about Christian Socialism – a sentiment agreeably defined by Marx as 'the holy water with which the priest consecrates the heart-burnings of the aristocrat'. The attack on middle-class socialists, or more correctly on social reformers, is less remote. 'They wish for a bourgeoisie without a proletariat.' In their view, 'the bourgeois is a bourgeois – for the benefit of the working class'. Marx thought that this programme was impossible nonsense. In fact it describes most contemporary societies. Finally, with the Utopian Socialists, Marx was concerned to demonstrate his superior practicality. After all, there was a good deal of Utopianism in his own views. The difference, he claimed, was that previous Utopians had been dreamers; he knew how to get there.

There is a last kick of practicality in the cursory end-section on the relations of Communists with the various working-class parties. The answer is simple: they support every revolutionary movement in order to bring forward 'the property question, no matter what its degree of development at the time'. In other words, democrats and nationalists were to be taken for a socialist ride, even in countries which were not ripe for socialism – the old logical contradiction raising its head once more. The paragraph on Germany is peculiarly interesting. One may suspect that the Communists, in Marx's words, 'turn their attention chiefly to Germany', because he was a German and was writing for German tailors. But he provides more general explanations. Germany, it seems, was more advanced than England had been in the seventeenth or France in the eighteenth century; therefore 'the bourgeois revolution will be but the prelude to an immediately following proletarian revolution'. This prophecy proved incorrect so far as Germany was concerned, but it came surprisingly to life during the Russian revolution of 1917. The last sentence of the *Manifesto* is as good as the first. It has in English no agreed form. The literal translation from the German would be: 'Proletarians of all lands, unite.' Samuel Moore, with Engels's approval, rendered it: 'Working men of all countries, unite!' The most common form has become: 'Workers of the world, unite!' Whatever the precise form, the sentiment is unmistakeable and powerful, though usually not powerful enough.

Such is *The Communist Manifesto,* a strange compound, like most sacred books, of the universal and the particular. It was written for an immediate, practical purpose, as a prelude to action during the revolutions of 1848. This practical purpose was not achieved. No revolutionaries of importance read the *Manifesto*, and none of them acted according to its instructions except perhaps Marx himself. The *Manifesto* has no relevance in the historical literature of the 1848 revolutions. In longer perspective, it is more important than all the writings produced in 1848, other than Tocqueville's *Memoirs*, and its publication was more important than any of the practical events. The *Manifesto* contains nearly all the elements which were to make Marxism the last and most contemporary of the great religions. It provided both a system of historical development and a programme for political action. It demonstrated that capitalism would inevitably be overthrown by socialism and laid down, rather less clearly, how the proletariat could bring this overthrow about.

Christianity, it is said, brought hope and consolation to the slaves of the Roman Empire. Marxism did much the same for the wage slaves of capitalism and indeed went one better. They did not need to wait for the next world. *The Communist Manifesto* assured them that they would win in this one.

The Communist Manifesto was not of course the final statement of Marx's creed. He lived for another thirty-five years, during which time he wrote many books and articles and was often politically active. Though he never openly abandoned any part of his system, he elaborated a good deal and modified more with the passage of time – thus unconsciously acknowledging his own principle that ideas grow out of the surrounding circumstances. His philosophical outlook remained Hegelian in form. Even here he slipped a little. He claimed that Darwin had done for biology what he himself had done for the social sciences and actually sent Darwin a copy of *Capital*. Darwinian evolution is a long way from the Hegelian process. If Marx really accepted it, then he had ceased to hold a revolutionary philosophy. Perhaps what he liked in Darwinianism was the survival of the fittest, which he regarded as a biological confirmation of the class struggle.

Marx's elaboration was greater in economic questions. He was not satisfied with the crude explanation, which Engels had picked up from routine English economists, that over-production was the cause of capitalist crises. Over-production was part of the crisis. Marx wanted to know why it happened. This was the theme of his major work, *Capital,* and Marx regarded his discovery of the cause of crisis as his greatest theoretical achievement. Unfortunately his discovery rests on the assumption, then held by all economists, that 'labour' was the source of 'value'. This assumption is no longer academically respectable. However, once it is accepted, the structure which Marx erected upon it is ingenious. The 'value' of any article is the socially-necessary labour-time required to produce it. The working man sells his labour-power for its full 'value' – that is, for the wages required to produce him again next day. But he produces more than his 'value'. This is surplus value, which the capitalist naturally appropriates. Thus the worker is robbed at the point of production without any evil intent on the part of the capitalist. The surplus value cannot be disposed of except to other capitalists, unless it is sent off outside the capitalist world. Ultimately the capitalists are choked by the surplus value which they cannot help accumulating. These ideas, when given a different theoretical dress, are not very different from those later formulated by J. M. Keynes. The difference lies in the solution. Keynes thought that an enlightened liberal state could compel the bloated capitalists to disgorge. Marx held that a working-class revolution or at any rate the dictatorship of the proletariat would be necessary.

On a more practical level, Marx gradually retreated from his conviction that the final crisis of capitalism was close at hand. He had expected this final crisis in 1848. When it failed to happen, he continued to hope that the next crisis would do the trick. An economic crisis duly occurred in 1857. It had no political consequence whatever. This was for Marx the moment of dis-illusion. He now recognized that capitalism had a long life before it, both by intensifying exploitation in each country and by extending its operations throughout the world. He did not live to see the next great crisis which came only in 1886. This, too, passed over without any revolutionary result. Engels, the surviving high-priest of Marxism, shifted his ground in his last years and expected the final crisis to be produced by war be-tween the Great Powers. The two alternative explanations were presented to Marxists of the twentieth century. They were tied together when Marxists discovered, before and during the first World war, that wars were themselves caused by capitalism. This discovery was not made by Marx, though he would no doubt have welcomed it.

Marx's greatest elaboration came on the political side. When he wrote the *Manifesto,* he had before him only the example of the great French revolution and foretold that the coming revo-lutions would be much the same – the simple seizure of power after a few days. The events of 1848 convinced him that this was totally inadequate. The proletariat could not take over the existing bourgeois state. They must destroy it and start afresh with a state which sprang from their own institutions. He de-veloped this view theoretically in the brilliant commentaries which he wrote on the French revolution of 1848 – *Class Struggles in France* and *The Eighteenth Brumaire of Louis Napoleon.* He claimed to have found concrete justification for his view in the Paris Commune of 1871. This, he announced, was the model for the proletarian state of the future. It does not matter that few of the Communards were Marxists, and even these few did not follow Marx's policy.

The Commune was not however Marx's only political legacy nor, so it seemed for many years, his important one. In many of his utterances, he gradually gave up his entire revolutionary approach, though without ever admitting that he had done so. The economic revolution which he postulated was really a figure of speech and not, in the ordinary sense, a revolution at all. It was rather a slow transformation of institutions and therewith of ideas which would take decades or even centuries.

A straight political revolution was no doubt necessary where the people did not have the vote. But, once there was universal suffrage, this political revolution had already happened. Even before Marx's death, universal suffrage was established in France and Germany, and there was household suffrage in Great Britain. The workers could conquer power by constitutional means. Marx himself said that the socialist revolution might happen peacefully in Great Britain, the United States, and perhaps Holland. Engels, later on, even added Germany. Violence might come only from the propertied classes who would refuse to be dispossessed peacefully. The contradiction between the two concepts of the revolutionary Commune and evolution based on universal suffrage was never clarified by Marx and Engels. The two ideas ran side by side. Some Marxists, a minority, continued to look forward to a violent revolution. Others, equally orthodox, placed their faith in what Sidney Webb, ostensibly a non-Marxist, called 'the inevitability of gradualness.' The only ones who did not have to worry were the Russians, faced, as they were, with a despotic tsar, and even they had to worry in 1917, when the first revolution of that year made universal suffrage theoretically possible.

Perhaps Marx's greatest political legacy was practical, and not in the field of theory at all – a view which would not have been altogether unwelcome to him as a thwarted man of action. This legacy was his insistence on working-class independence in political affairs, with a clear working-class programme and working-class leaders. Marx did more than preach this. He practised it when he created, almost single-handed, the First International or, to give its full name, the International Working Men's Association. Marx's International was more formidable in appearance than in reality. At its most successful, it had only two hundred and ninety four individual members, and the affiliated societies were mostly small English trade unions whose leaders little understood what they were committed to. The International caused much alarm to the conservative governments of Europe. It was torn by internal dissension and broke up when Marx insisted on championing the Paris Commune. But it demonstrated his principle that the emancipation of the working class must be the work of the working class themselves. Every Labour and Socialist party in the world stems from the example which Marx set, even though they often repudiate the rest of his teaching.

There were other and less fortunate examples which Marx set in the International. He had declared in *The Communist Manifesto* that enlightened bourgeois thinkers, who understood the process of history, would go over to the working-class side. Marx was the living proof of his own statement. He was a bourgeois thinker, none more so, who had joined the working-class and had indeed claimed to lead it. But he could endure no rival near the throne. Other bourgeois thinkers who tried to enter the working-class movement encountered Marx's relentless hostility. Marx denounced their theories and, if this were not enough, discredited them by underhand means. He fought Lassalle in the German movement and even used anti-semitic prejudice against him, regardless of the fact that Marx himself was of Jewish origin. He fought Bakunin in the International and finally killed it rather than allow him to exercise any influence. Marx's picture of the working-class movement was of subservient and rather stupid workingmen doing exactly what Marx told them. This picture was already implicit in *The Communist Manifesto*. The Communists were those who knew what was best for the working class. In 1847 the Communists were limited to Marx and Engels. Later Communist leaders, themselves nearly all of bourgeois origin, made the same claim. In Hegelian terms, there was a conflict between the great unconscious working-class movement and its conscious bourgeois leaders. Marx did not discover a happy synthesis between these conflicting forces, and no one has done so since.

The Communist Manifesto has had a long run. Its doctrines have been tested by a hundred and twenty years of history, during which time men have often tried to put them into practice. Some of the *Manifesto* has been triumphantly vindicated. Nearly everyone now accepts the principle that ideas and beliefs grow out of and reflect existing society rather than lead an independent life. Even here there was a hole in the Marxist system. Men have often dedicated their lives to ideals which have very little to do with surrounding circumstances, to the ideal, say, of Justice or Freedom. Marx can be said to have done this himself. There is something lacking in a philosophy which allows no place for its originator. What economic need was Marx serving when he sat for long hours at a desk in the British Museum or attended hole-and-corner meetings of half a dozen obscure men? He was asserting his personality, and this, rather than class conflict, has often been the driving force of history.

Marx was right when he foretold the development of capitalism and of the proletariat. He failed to grasp the complexity of this development. The primitive capitalism of Marx's time worked in a primitive way. Individual capitalists mostly owned the cotton mills, and many of them believed, though some of the greatest did not, that they could prosper only if they compelled their employees to work long hours for low wages. Capitalism of this kind survives now only in backward communities. The limited company has taken the place of the individual owner in all great undertakings. There has been a divorce between ownership and control, which is altogether beyond Marx's system. The profit motive has ceased to be the only driving force of capitalism, or even the principal one. The shareholders no doubt want profits when they are allowed to take them. The managers and directors are concerned far more with efficient working and only make enough profit to keep the shareholders quiet. As in other walks of life, power has become more important than profit, a calculation which hardly entered into Marx's system.

On the other hand, capitalism has not had the steamroller effect which Marx expected. It is not true that everyone except a few capitalists is being forced into the ranks of the proletariat. Quite the contrary. The proletariat has tended to remain a static element in society, or even to decline. Marx in his analysis never seems to acknowledge the middlemen and administrators who make capitalism work. The more capitalism flourishes, the more there are of them. Advanced capitalism has brought with it an increasing middle class, so much so that one can imagine it without individual capitalists at all. Only then it is called state capitalism, a system which apparently operates in Soviet Russia. Those who run things are the real rulers of society, and there is far more to run than there was before. The proletariat has not much increased its proportion of numbers in the community and is no nearer running things than it ever was.

It is a grave upset to the Marxist system that the proletariat has not become the ruling class in the community and shows no sign of doing so. There is an even graver upset. Increasing prosperity for the capitalists has everywhere brought with it increasing prosperity for the proletariat, instead of the increasing misery which Marx foretold. The most advanced capitalist countries are also those where the working class has the highest standard of life. The failure of the law of increasing misery has worried Marxists for a long time. When this failure first became obvious, towards the end of the nineteenth century, some Marxists devised the explanation of imperialist super-profit. The capitalists of the highly advanced countries were taking, as it were, an unfair advantage of the rest of the world and were passing on a small share of the loot to their own working class. Many capitalists themselves believed this, or at any rate the advocates of imperialism did so. More recently, the imperial powers have all lost their empires. As a result they have become more prosperous than they were before. Everyone knows, for instance, that the British working class would be better off if the British government did not insist on clinging to the tattered remnants of a dead Empire. Imperialist super-profit has not proved a good bet or a good explanation.

Most Marxists have been content to deny that the workers were becoming more prosperous or else to assert that the prosperity would be short-lived. John Strachey tried a different explanation. He was one of the few original Marxist thinkers, perhaps the only one produced in England. He began, like Marx himself, by announcing the coming crisis of capitalism. When his prophecy also proved incorrect, he thought again. According to him, the workers had been able to defeat the law of increasing misery, thanks to the strength of their trade-union and other organizations. Marx had already remarked on this, when he instanced the victory over the Ten Hour Bill in England, though he had not allowed this to shake his system. Strachey however held that all the workings of capitalism were being modified, beneficently of course, by working-class pressure. This was true, but it was not the whole truth. No doubt the workers insisted on higher wages and shorter hours. But many capitalists came to take the same line, perhaps to their own surprise. The more prosperous the workers were, the more they could buy and the greater capitalist profits became. Successful industries are high-wage industries, and successful capitalist economies are high-wage countries. Every advance in capitalism pushes up wages, and every increase in wages pushes up profits. Some capitalists went on behaving stupidly, as Marx expected them to do, and did not see further than the end of their noses. In general capitalists have behaved sensibly even when they did not know what they were doing. Higher wages are in fact not a contradiction of capitalism, or a defeat for it. On the contrary, they protect capitalism and actually make it work better.

Here is the reason why another essential prophecy of Marx's has not been fulfilled. Capitalist crises have not become worse. They have grown less frequent, less disastrous, and more easily overcome. There was one exception: the great Depression which devastated the world between 1929 and 1933. This began as a true crisis of the Marxist pattern: a financial crash in the United States, the most advanced capitalist country, which provoked unemployment throughout the world. The capitalists behaved in an old-fashioned way. They reduced wages in Germany and the United States and tried to do so in Great Britain. They thus succeeded in making the crisis worse. Marxists cheerfully announced that the final crisis had at last arrived. Instead governments spent their way out of the Depression, first in the United States and then more completely in Germany. When the British government failed to follow suit, individuals did the spending for them. The Depression passed over without a single Marxist revolution.

Indeed, very discouragingly for Marxists, revolutions have grown fewer, not more frequent, and the few revolutions have not followed the Marxist pattern. The revolutions of 1848, hailed by Marx as the first of a series, proved to be the last so far as most of Europe was concerned. There was national unification in Germany from above, and national unification in Italy after revolutions of a modest kind. Napoleon III was overthrown in France, rather because of military defeat than by a revolution, and a republic was established. Otherwise there were no more European revolutions of any significance until the end of the first World war. This was expected to produce universal Marxist, or as they were then called Bolshevik, revolutions. It duly produced one in Russia. This was the most backward capitalist country in Europe, not the most advanced, and the revolution owed its survival to the support of the peasantry, more than of the proletariat. Apart from this, there was again no revolution of any significant kind.

The end of the second World war was even more surprising. The second war had been even more destructive than the first. Yet there was little social disturbance and no Communist revolution at all except in the entirely peasant country of Yugoslavia. Even the countries liberated by the Soviet armies did not become Communist until later, when they were forced into Communist rule by the needs of the Cold War. The aftermath of the second World war saw one substantial Communist victory, as great perhaps as the original Bolshevik victory in Russia. This was the establishment of a Communist China. War, as earlier in Russia, had merely helped to finish off a decadent regime. More than this, the Chinese Communists won in an almost entirely peasant country and almost entirely thanks to peasant support. One Marxist writer has commented on the fact, bewildering to him, that the Chinese Communists actually became stronger when the Japanese conquest of the seaboard destroyed the movement of the industrial workers. This is not really bewildering. Peasants, it seems, make revolutions. The proletariat do not. Or, to imitate Marx in a still more sweeping generalization, revolutions occur in backward countries, not in advanced ones. Hence, with the advance of capitalism, the twentieth century has been singularly free from social revolutions – against all expectations.

Earlier in the century, and particularly in the thirties, there were revolutions of a non-Marxist kind. These were the Fascist revolutions, which claimed to set a new pattern in history, though Fascism seems in fact to have sunk without trace. Marx had foretold such revolutions in *The Communist Manifesto*: an alliance between the *Lumpenproletariat* and the lower middle class, and from which the capitalists were supposed to benefit. They appeared a sham to Marxist eyes, though they were real enough for those who experienced them. Once more other classes were more revolutionary than the industrial working class. Indeed, the industrial workers were predominantly a stable, conservative element, particularly in Germany, and the better organized they were, the more conservative they became. In every country, industrial workers were least responsive to the appeal of Fascism, and this not because they wanted a revolution of their own. The Fascist leaders, on the other hand, were exactly of the type which Marx had postulated as leaders for the proletariat, including even bourgeois ideologists, who thought they knew how history was going. It only needed a spin of the coin to determine whether Mussolini would be a Communist or a Fascist, and, though Hitler never had Marxist leanings, he would have been at home a century earlier with the exiled tailors of the German Educational Workers' League.

The proletariat have been the great disappointment in the Marxist system and have upset its workings. Marx, who probably never encountered a true proletarian in his life, thought that the proletariat would want power, as presumably he did. But power is an itch suffered, fortunately, by comparatively few men. Even the bourgeoisie, whom Marx regarded as greedy for power, often let it slide. Bright and Cobden complained during Marx's lifetime that the English bourgeoisie were content to leave power in the hands of Palmerston and other aristocrats instead of grasping it themselves. Power brings responsibility with it, and most men do not want responsibility. They want a comfortable life for themselves and their families. They may be driven into action if public affairs are mismanaged, though even then they put up with a great deal. In normal times, they are delighted that others are running affairs for them – the employer in the factory, the politician in the state. Class consciousness can well exist without class war. In any case, even class consciousness is disappearing with the general levelling of culture – a levelling which has little to do with changes in the system of production.

Revolutions in short are made in the name of the proletariat, not by it, and usually in countries where the proletariat hardly exists. What is more, these revolutions do not bring the triumph or dictatorship of the proletariat. They bring the dictatorship of a new managerial class, or sometimes of the old class under a new name. In any society, a few men will aspire to run things, and the great majority will allow them to do it. A very important element in Marx's system, perhaps the most important, was the self-confidence which it inspired in the managers. The Communists, from Marx onwards, were the chosen few who really knew what the proletariat wanted. They knew only because they said they knew. This was enough to convince them that they would always be right. Someone called Marxists 'God's prompters'. Lenin was the most confident and persistent of these prompters. He laid down, according to Marx's own pattern, that, since he was always right, the ideal Communist party should be composed of men strictly subordinate to his orders. Shortly before the Bolshevik revolution, he produced a rather duller version of *The Communist Manifesto*, entitled *The State and Revolution*. There were enough parallels between Europe in 1848 and Russia in 1917 to make Lenin's adaptation plausible. There was again a bourgeois democratic revolution which Lenin proposed to take over for proletarian purposes. Unlike Marx, Lenin succeeded. But he saved his revolution by perpetuating the peasantry, a class which Marx said was doomed to disappear. Lenin announced the dictatorship of the proletariat. He also followed Marx and declared that the proletarian state would soon 'wither away'. This prophecy has not been fulfilled. Instead there has been a dictatorship of the Communist party over the proletariat and the dictatorship of a few individuals, or sometimes of a single man, over the Communist party.

As with every religious book, men can find in *The Com-*

munist Manifesto whatever they want to find. Some bourgeois ideologists and perhaps even some proletarians still find in it the promise of a coming revolution. Others find the assurance that Utopia will arrive inevitably – Engels's word – of itself. Events are still forced into its pattern or written off if they turn out recalcitrant. Many things are still held to be true because Marx stated or 'proved' them.

What strikes a historian on the other hand is how deeply *The Communist Manifesto* is rooted in the circumstances of its time. It generalizes from the economic crisis of 1847 and from the coming revolutions of 1848. It reflects, with a sharpness all its own, what many men were thinking in a more confused way during the eighteen forties. The class conflict and the misery of the proletariat were then observed facts. Marx seemed to his contemporaries a subversive writer, challenging accepted habits of thought. In retrospect he appears as a respectable Victorian gentleman of scholarly disposition, much given, as many Victorians were, to knowing what was good for his intellectual inferiors. His outlook was much the same as Macaulay's, except that Macaulay thought that Utopia had already arrived with the triumph of the bourgeoisie, whereas Marx expected the same result from the triumph of the proletariat. Marx, like most of his contemporaries, was a dogmatic optimist. He was convinced that events moved always towards the victory of the Higher. This faith in an inevitable outcome made him a great religious teacher. The inevitable rarely happens in real life.

Bibliography

THE full bibliographical history of the *Manifesto* is to be found in *Le Manifeste Communiste* by Bert Andréas (Milan, 1963). This lists 544 items, mostly editions of the *Manifesto*, which appeared between 1848 and 1918, and a further 218 editions which appeared between 1919 and 1959. The manuscript of the *Manifesto* has not survived, except for a single sheet, now in the Marx-Engels-Lenin Institute in Moscow, which Engels gave to Wilhelm Liebknecht at the time of Marx's death in 1883. The first edition (in German) was published in February 1848 at the office of the 'Bildungsgesellschaft für Arbeiter', 46 Liverpool Street, Bishopsgate, by J. E. Burghard. This description is misleading. The office of the *Gesellschaft* was in High Holborn. It seems that the *Gesellschaft* had recently imported Gothic type from Germany and, not possessing a press of its own, employed Burghard as printer. The first edition had numerous proof-reading errors. A corrected edition came out in April or May, and all later German editions derive from it. The corrections were made by the printer, not by Marx or Engels, both of whom displayed a curious indifference to the printed version of their most famous work.

The French translation of 1848, to which Engels refers in his introductions, did not in fact appear. The only translation published in 1848 – or at any rate the only one which has survived – was into Swedish. Engels also got the details of the Russian translation wrong. The first translation by Bakunin came out in 1869, not in the early sixties. The second translation was by Plekhanov, not by Vera Zasulich. The first English translation, by Helen Macfarlane, appeared in the columns of Harney's *Red Republican* in 1850. This translation was reproduced in New York in 1871. The English translation in common use was made in 1888 by Samuel Moore, the translator of *Capital* This translation, based on the German edition of 1872, was supervised by Engels, who also contributed some notes. Another translation by Eden and Cedar Paul was published by Martin Lawrence in 1930. Though often more idiomatic than Moore's translation, it is less familiar than his. This edition also contains the catechism by Engels and an introduction, giving the history of the *Manifesto*, by D. Riazanoff, then director of the Marx-Engels Institute. In all, the *Manifesto* has been translated into thirty languages, including Esperanto. Andréas gives a facsimile reproduction of the first German edition. It occupies twenty-three pages.

There is an interesting, though now somewhat dated, commentary by Charles Andler in French (1902). Harold Laski produced an edition with a hundred-page introduction (1948), in which he demonstrated that the contemporary Labour government in Great Britain came nearest to Marx's ideal. The standard life of Marx is by Franz Mehring (1918, abbreviated English translation 1936), and of Engels by G. Mayer (1934, abbreviated English translation 1936). The most useful English life is by E. H. Carr (1934). Works on Marxism are divided, as are works on all great religions, into those by believers and those by non-believers. The works by believers are incomprehensible to non-believers, and no doubt the other way round. To a non-believer, the most dispassionate appear to be *Marx: His Time and Ours* by R. Schlesinger (1950); *A History of Socialist Thought*, volume 1, by G. D. H. Cole (1953); *German Marxism and Russian Communism* by John Plamenatz (1954), and *Marxism* by George Lichtheim (1961).

The edition of the *Manifesto* which follows is a reproduction of the translation made by Samuel Moore in 1888 from the original German text of 1848 and revised by Friedrich Engels. Included are Engel's annotations for the English 1888 edition and the German 1890 edition, and the authors' prefaces to the various editions.

PREFACES

Preface to the
German Edition of 1872

THE Communist League, an international association of workers, which could of course be only a secret one under the conditions obtaining at the time, commissioned the undersigned, at the Congress held in London in November, 1847, to draw up for publication a detailed theoretical and practical programme of the Party.[1]* Such was the origin of the following Manifesto, the manuscript of which travelled to London, to be printed, a few weeks before the February Revolution.[2] First published in German, it has been republished in that language in at least twelve different editions in Germany, England and America. It was published in English for the first time in 1850 in the *Red Republican*, London, translated by Miss Helen Macfarlane, and in 1871 in at least three different translations in America. A French version first appeared in Paris shortly before the June insurrection of 1848[3] and recently in *Le Socialiste* of New York. A new translation is in the course of preparation. A Polish version appeared in London shortly after it was first published in German. A Russian translation was published in Geneva in the sixties. Into Danish, too, it was translated shortly after its first appearance.

However much the state of things may have altered during the last twenty-five years, the general principles laid down in this Manifesto are, on the whole, as correct today as ever. Here and there some detail might be improved. The practical application of the principles will depend, as the Manifesto itself states, everywhere and at all times, on the historical conditions for the time being existing, and, for that reason, no special stress is laid on the revolutionary

*For numbered notes, by A. J. P. Taylor, see page 123.

measures proposed at the end of Section II. That passage would, in many respects, be very differently worded today. In view of the gigantic strides of Modern Industry in the last twenty-five years, and of the accompanying improved and extended party organization of the working class, in view of the practical experience gained, first in the February Revolution, and then, still more, in the Paris Commune, where the proletariat for the first time held political power for two whole months, this programme has in some details become antiquated.⁴ One thing especially was proved by the Commune, viz., that 'the working class cannot simply lay hold of the ready-made State machinery, and wield it for its own purposes'. (See *The Civil War in France; Address of the General Council of the International Working Men's Association*, London, Truelove, 1871, p. 15, where this point is further developed.) Further, it is self-evident that the criticism of Socialist literature is deficient in relation to the present time, because it comes down only to 1847; also that the remarks on the relation of the Communists to the various opposition parties (Section IV), although in principle still correct, yet in practice are antiquated, because the political situation has been entirely changed, and the progress of history has swept from off the earth the greater portion of the political parties there enumerated.

But, then, the Manifesto has become a historical document which we have no longer any right to alter. A subsequent edition may perhaps appear with an introduction bridging the gap from 1847 to the present day; this reprint was too unexpected to leave us time for that.

London, 24 June 1872   KARL MARX
                              FREDERICK ENGELS

Preface to the
Russian Edition of 1882

THE first Russian edition of the *Manifesto of the Communist Party*, translated by Bakunin, was published early in the sixties by the printing office of the *Kolokol*. Then the West could see in it (the *Russian* edition of the Manifesto) only a literary curiosity. Such a view would be impossible today.

What a limited field the proletarian movement still occupied at that time (December 1847) is most clearly shown by the last section of the Manifesto: the position of the Communists in relation to the various opposition parties in the various countries. Precisely Russia and the United States are missing here. It was the time when Russia constituted the last great reserve of all European reaction, when the United States absorbed the surplus proletarian forces of Europe through immigration. Both countries provided Europe with raw materials and were at the same time markets for the sale of its industrial products. At that time both were, therefore, in one way or another, pillars of the existing European order.

How very different today! Precisely European immigration fitted North America for a gigantic agricultural production, whose competition is shaking the very foundations of European landed property – large and small. In addition it enabled the United States to exploit its tremendous industrial resources with an energy and on a scale that must shortly break the industrial monopoly of Western Europe, and especially of England, existing up to now. Both circumstances react in revolutionary manner upon America itself. Step by step the small and middle landownership of the farmers, the basis of the whole political constitution, is succumbing to the competition of giant farms; simultaneously, a mass proletariat and a fabulous concentration of capitals are developing for the first time in the industrial regions.

And now Russia! During the Revolution of 1848–49 not only the European princes, but the European bourgeois as well, found their only salvation from the proletariat, just beginning to awaken, in Russian intervention. The tsar was proclaimed the chief of European reaction. Today he is a prisoner of war of the revolution, in Gatchina,[5] and Russia forms the vanguard of revolutionary action in Europe.

The Communist Manifesto had as its object the proclamation of the inevitably impending dissolution of modern bourgeois property. But in Russia we find, face to face with the rapidly developing capitalist swindle and bourgeois landed property, just beginning to develop, more than half the land owned in common by the peasants. Now the question is: can the Russian *obshchina*, though greatly undermined, yet a form of the primeval common ownership of land, pass directly to the higher form of communist common ownership? Or on the contrary, must it first pass through the same process of dissolution as constitutes the historical evolution of the West?

The only answer to that possible today is this: If the Russian Revolution becomes the signal for a proletarian revolution in the West, so that both complement each other, the present Russian common ownership of land may serve as the starting point for a communist development.

London, 21 January 1882   KARL MARX
                                   FREDERICK ENGELS

Preface to the German Edition of 1883

THE preface to the present edition I must, alas, sign alone. Marx – the man to whom the whole working class of Europe and America owes more than to anyone else – rests at Highgate Cemetery and over his grave the first grass is already growing. Since his death, there can be even less thought of revising or supplementing the Manifesto. All the more do I consider it necessary again to state here the following expressly:

The basic thought running through the Manifesto – that economic production and the structure of society of every historical epoch necessarily arising therefrom constitute the foundation for the political and intellectual history of that epoch; that consequently (ever since the dissolution of the primeval communal ownership of land) all history has been a history of class struggles, of struggles between exploited and exploiting, between dominated and dominating classes at various stages of social development; that this struggle, however, has now reached a stage where the exploited and oppressed class (the proletariat) can no longer emancipate itself from the class which exploits and oppresses it (the bourgeoisie), without at the same time for ever freeing the whole of society from exploitation, oppression and class struggles – this basic thought belongs solely and exclusively to Marx.*

* 'This proposition,' I wrote in the preface to the English translation, 'which, in my opinion, is destined to do for history what Darwin's theory has done for biology, we, both of us, had been gradually approaching for some years before 1845. How far I had independently progressed towards it, is best shown by my *Condition of the Working Class in England*. But when I again met Marx at Brussels, in spring, 1845, he had it ready worked out, and put it before me, in terms almost as clear as those in which I have stated it here.' [*Note by Engels to the German edition of 1890*.]

I have already stated this many times; but precisely now it is necessary that it also stand in front of the Manifesto itself.

London, 28 June 1883   F. ENGELS

Preface to the
English Edition of 1888

THE Manifesto was published as the platform of the 'Communist League', a working men's association, first exclusively German, later on international, and, under the political conditions of the Continent before 1848, unavoidably a secret society. At a Congress of the League, held in London in November, 1847, Marx and Engels were commissioned to prepare for publication a complete theoretical and practical party programme. Drawn up in German, in January, 1848, the manuscript was sent to the printer in London a few weeks before the French revolution of February 24th. A French translation was brought out in Paris, shortly before the insurrection of June, 1848. The first English translation, by Miss Helen Macfarlane, appeared in George Julian Harney's *Red Republican*, London, 1850. A Danish and a Polish edition had also been published.

The defeat of the Parisian insurrection of June, 1848 – the first great battle between Proletariat and Bourgeoisie – drove again into the background, for a time, the social and political aspirations of the European working class. Thenceforth, the struggle for supremacy was again, as it had been before the revolution of February, solely between different sections of the propertied class; the working class was reduced to a fight for political elbow-room, and to the position of extreme wing of the middle-class Radicals. Wherever independent proletarian movements continued to show signs of life, they were ruthlessly hunted down. Thus the Prussian police hunted out the Central Board of the Communist League, then located in Cologne. The members were arrested, and, after eighteen months' imprisonment, they were tried in October, 1852. This celebrated 'Cologne

Communist trial' lasted from October 4th till November 12th; seven of the prisoners were sentenced to terms of imprisonment in a fortress, varying from three to six years. Immediately after the sentence, the League was formally dissolved by the remaining members. As to the Manifesto, it seemed thenceforth to be doomed to oblivion.

When the European working class had recovered sufficient strength for another attack on the ruling classes, the International Working Men's Association sprang up. But this association, formed with the express aim of welding into one body the whole militant proletariat of Europe and America, could not at once proclaim the principles laid down in the Manifesto. The International was bound to have a programme broad enough to be acceptable to the English Trades Unions, to the followers of Proudhon in France, Belgium, Italy, and Spain, and to the Lassalleans* in Germany. Marx who drew up this programme to the satisfaction of all parties, entirely trusted to the intellectual development of the working class, which was sure to result from combined action and mutual discussion. The very events and vicissitudes of the struggle against Capital, the defeats even more than the victories, could not help bringing home to men's minds the insufficiency of their various favourite nostrums, and preparing the way for a more complete insight into the true conditions of working-class emancipation. And Marx was right. The International, on its breaking up in 1874, left the workers quite different men from what it had found them in 1864. Proudhonism in France, Lassalleanism in Germany were dying out, and even the conservative English Trades Unions, though most of

* Lassalle personally, to us, always acknowledged himself to be a disciple of Marx, and, as such, stood on the ground of the Manifesto. But in his public agitation, 1862–4, he did not go beyond demanding cooperative workshops supported by state credit. [*Note by Engels.*]

them had long since severed their connexion with the International, were gradually advancing towards that point at which, last year at Swansea, their President could say in their name 'Continental Socialism has lost its terrors for us'. In fact: the principles of the Manifesto had made considerable headway among the working men of all countries.

The Manifesto itself thus came to the front again. The German text had been, since 1850, reprinted several times in Switzerland, England and America. In 1872, it was translated into English in New York, where the translation was published in *Woodhull and Claflin's Weekly*. From this English version, a French one was made in *Le Socialiste* of New York. Since then at least two more English translations, more or less mutilated, have been brought out in America, and one of them has been reprinted in England. The first Russian translation, made by Bakunin, was published at Herzen's *Kolokol* office in Geneva, about 1863; a second one, by the heroic Vera Zasulich, also in Geneva, 1882. A new Danish edition is to be found in *Social-demokratisk Bibliothek*, Copenhagen, 1885; a fresh French translation in *Le Socialiste*, Paris 1885. From this latter a Spanish version was prepared and published in Madrid, 1886. The German reprints are not to be counted, there have been twelve altogether at the least. An Armenian translation, which was to be published in Constantinople some months ago, did not see the light, I am told, because the publisher was afraid of bringing out a book with the name of Marx on it, while the translator declined to call it his own production. Of further translations into other languages I have heard, but have not seen them. Thus the history of the Manifesto reflects, to a great extent, the history of the modern working-class movement; at present it is undoubtedly the most widespread, the most international production of all Socialist literature, the common platform acknowledged by millions of working men from Siberia to California.

Yet, when it was written, we could not have called it a *Socialist* Manifesto. By Socialists, in 1847, were understood, on the one hand, the adherents of the various Utopian systems: Owenites in England, Fourierists in France, both of them already reduced to the position of mere sects, and gradually dying out; on the other hand, the most multifarious social quacks, who, by all manners of tinkering, professed to redress, without any danger to capital and profit, all sorts of social grievances; in both cases men outside the working-class movement, and looking rather to the 'educated' classes for support. Whatever portion of the working class had become convinced of the insufficiency of mere political revolutions, and had proclaimed the necessity of a total social change, that portion then called itself Communist. It was a crude, rough-hewn, purely instinctive sort of Communism; still, it touched the cardinal point and was powerful enough amongst the working class to produce the Utopian Communism, in France, of Cabet, and in Germany, of Weitling. Thus, Socialism was, in 1847, a middle-class movement, Communism, a working-class movement. Socialism was, on the Continent at least, 'respectable'; Communism was the very opposite. And as our notion, from the very beginning, was that 'the emancipation of the working class must be the act of the working class itself', there could be no doubt as to which of the two names we must take. Moreover, we have, ever since, been far from repudiating it.

The Manifesto being our joint production, I consider myself bound to state that the fundamental proposition, which forms its nucleus, belongs to Marx. That proposition is: that in every historical epoch, the prevailing mode of economic production and exchange, and the social organization necessarily following from it, form the basis upon which is built up, and from which alone can be explained, the political and intellectual history of that epoch; that consequently the whole history of mankind (since the dissolution of primitive tribal society, holding land in common ownership) has been a history of class struggles, contests between exploiting and exploited, ruling and oppressed classes; that the history of these class struggles forms a series of evolutions in which, nowadays, a stage has been reached where the exploited and oppressed class – the proletariat – cannot attain its emancipation from the sway of the exploiting and ruling class – the bourgeoisie – without, at the same time, and once and for all, emancipating society at large from all exploitation, oppression, class distinctions and class struggles.

This proposition which, in my opinion, is destined to do for history what Darwin's theory has done for biology, we, both of us, had been gradually approaching for some years before 1845. How far I had independently progressed towards it, is best shown by my *Condition of the Working Class in England*.* But when I again met Marx at Brussels, in spring, 1845, he had it ready worked out, and put it before me, in terms almost as clear as those in which I have stated it here.

From our joint preface to the German edition of 1872, I quote the following:

'However much the state of things may have altered during the last twenty-five years, the general principles laid down in this Manifesto are, on the whole, as correct today as ever. Here and there some detail might be improved. The practical application of the principles will depend, as the Manifesto itself states, everywhere and at all times, on the historical conditions for the time being existing, and, for that reason, no special stress is laid on the revolutionary measures proposed at the end of Section II. That passage

The Condition of the Working Class in England in 1844. By Frederick Engels. Translated by Florence K. Wischnewetzky, New York. Lovell – London. W. Reeves, 1888. [*Note by Engels.*]

would, in many respects, be very differently worded today. In view of the gigantic strides of Modern Industry since 1848, and of the accompanying improved and extended organization of the working class, in view of the practical experience gained, first in the February Revolution, and then, still more, in the Paris Commune, where the proletariat for the first time held political power for two whole months, this programme has in some details become antiquated. One thing especially was proved by the Commune, viz., that "the working class cannot simply lay hold of the ready-made State machinery, and wield it for its own purposes". (See *The Civil War in France; Address of the General Council of the International Working Men's Association*, London, Truelove, 1871, p. 15, where this point is further developed.) Further, it is self-evident that the criticism of Socialist literature is deficient in relation to the present time, because it comes down only to 1847; also, that the remarks on the relation of the Communists to the various opposition parties (Section IV), although in principle still correct, yet in practice are antiquated, because the political situation has been entirely changed, and the progress of history has swept from off the earth the greater portion of the political parties there enumerated.

'But then, the Manifesto has become a historical document which we have no longer any right to alter.'

The present translation is by Mr Samuel Moore, the translator of the greater portion of Marx's *Capital*. We have revised it in common, and I have added a few notes explanatory of historical allusions.

London, 30 January 1888   F. ENGELS

Preface to the German Edition of 1890

SINCE the above was written,* a new German edition of the Manifesto has again become necessary, and much has also happened to the Manifesto which should be recorded here.

A second Russian translation – by Vera Zasulich – appeared at Geneva in 1882; the preface to that edition was written by Marx and myself. Unfortunately, the original German manuscript has gone astray; I must therefore retranslate from the Russian, which will in no way improve the text. It reads:

'The first Russian edition of the *Manifesto of the Communist Party*, translated by Bakunin, was published early in the sixties by the printing office of the *Kolokol*. Then the West could see in it (the Russian edition of the Manifesto) only a literary curiosity. Such a view would be impossible today.

'What a limited field the proletarian movement still occupied at that time (December 1847) is most clearly shown by the last section of the Manifesto: the position of the Communists in relation to the various opposition parties in the various countries. Precisely Russia and the United States are missing here. It was the time when Russia constituted the last great reserve of all European reaction, when the United States absorbed the surplus proletarian forces of Europe through immigration. Both countries provided Europe with raw materials and were at the same time markets for the sale of its industrial products. At that time both were, therefore, in one way or another, pillars of the existing European order.

*Engels is referring to his preface to the German edition of 1883.

'How very different today! Precisely European immigration fitted North America for a gigantic agricultural production, whose competition is shaking the very foundations of European landed property – large and small. In addition it enabled the United States to exploit its tremendous industrial resources with an energy and on a scale that must shortly break the industrial monopoly of Western Europe, and especially of England, existing up to now. Both circumstances react in revolutionary manner upon America itself. Step by step the small and middle landownership of the farmers, the basis of the whole political constitution, is succumbing to the competition of giant farms; simultaneously, a mass proletariat and a fabulous concentration of capitals are developing for the first time in the industrial regions.

'And now Russia! During the Revolution of 1848–49 not only the European princes, but the European bourgeois as well, found their only salvation from the proletariat, just beginning to awaken, in Russian intervention. The tsar was proclaimed the chief of European reaction. Today he is a prisoner of war of the revolution, in Gatchina, and Russia forms the vanguard of revolutionary action in Europe.

'The Communist Manifesto had as its object the proclamation of the inevitably impending dissolution of modern bourgeois property. But in Russia we find, face to face with the rapidly developing capitalist swindle and bourgeois landed property, just beginning to develop, more than half the land owned in common by the peasants. Now the question is: can the Russian *obshchina*, though greatly undermined, yet a form of the primeval common ownership of land, pass directly to the higher form of communist common ownership? Or on the contrary, must it first pass through the same process of dissolution as constitutes the historical evolution of the West?

'The only answer to that possible today is this: If the

Russian Revolution becomes the signal for a proletarian revolution in the West, so that both complement each other, the present Russian common ownership of land may serve as the starting point for a communist development.

'*London, 21 January 1882*   KARL MARX
FREDERICK ENGELS'

At about the same date, a new Polish version appeared in Geneva : *Manifest Komunistyczny*.

Furthermore, a new Danish translation has appeared in the *Social-demokratisk Bibliothek*, Copenhagen, 1885. Unfortunately it is not quite complete; certain essential passages, which seem to have presented difficulties to the translator, have been omitted, and in addition there are signs of carelessness here and there, which are all the more unpleasantly conspicuous since the translation indicates that had the translator taken a little more pains he would have done an excellent piece of work.

A new French version appeared in 1885 in *Le Socialiste* of Paris; it is the best published to date.

From this latter a Spanish version was published the same year, first in *El Socialista* of Madrid, and then reissued in pamphlet form : *Manifiesto del Partido Comunista* por Carlos Marx y F. Engels, Madrid, Administración de *El Socialista*, Hernán Cortés 8.

As a matter of curiosity I may also mention that in 1887 the manuscript of an Armenian translation was offered to a publisher in Constantinople. But the good man did not have the courage to publish something bearing the name of Marx and suggested that the translator set down his own name as author, which the latter, however, declined.

After one and then another of the more or less inaccurate American translations had been repeatedly reprinted in England, an authentic version at last appeared in 1888. This was by my friend Samuel Moore, and we went through it together once more before it was sent to press. It is entitled : *Manifesto of the Communist Party*, by Karl Marx and Frederick Engels. Authorized English Translation, edited and annotated by Frederick Engels, 1888. London, William Reeves, 185 Fleet st., E.C. I have added some of the notes of that edition to the present one.

The Manifesto has had a history of its own. Greeted with enthusiasm, at the time of its appearance, by the then still not at all numerous vanguard of scientific Socialism (as is proved by the translations mentioned in the first preface), it was soon forced into the background by the reaction that began with the defeat of the Paris workers in June 1848, and was finally excommunicated 'according to law' by the conviction of the Cologne Communists in November 1852. With the disappearance from the public scene of the workers' movement that had begun with the February Revolution, the Manifesto too passed into the background.

When the working class of Europe had again gathered sufficient strength for a new onslaught upon the power of the ruling classes, the International Working Men's Association came into being. Its aim was to weld together into *one* huge army the whole militant working class of Europe and America. Therefore it could not *set out* from the principles laid down in the Manifesto. It was bound to have a programme which would not shut the door on the English trade unions, the French, Belgian, Italian and Spanish Proudhonists and the German Lassalleans.* This programme – the preamble to the Rules of the International – was drawn

*Lassalle personally, to us, always acknowledged himself to be a 'disciple' of Marx, and, as such, stood, of course, on the ground of the Manifesto. Matters were quite different with regard to those of his followers who did not go beyond his demand for producers' cooperatives supported by state credits and who divided the whole working class into supporters of state assistance and supporters of self-assistance. [*Note by Engels.*]

up by Marx with a master hand acknowledged even by Bakunin and the Anarchists. For the ultimate triumph of the ideas set forth in the Manifesto Marx relied solely and exclusively upon the intellectual development of the working class, as it necessarily had to ensue from united action and discussion. The events and vicissitudes in the struggle against capital, the defeats even more than the successes, could not but demonstrate to the fighters the inadequacy hitherto of their universal panaceas and make their minds more receptive to a thorough understanding of the true conditions for the emancipation of the workers. And Marx was right. The working class of 1874, at the dissolution of the International, was altogether different from that of 1864, at its foundation. Proudhonism in the Latin countries and the specific Lassalleanism in Germany were dying out, and even the then arch-conservative English trade unions were gradually approaching the point where in 1887 the chairman of their Swansea Congress could say in their name 'Continental Socialism has lost its terrors for us'. Yet by 1887 Continental Socialism was almost exclusively the theory heralded in the Manifesto. Thus, to a certain extent, the history of the Manifesto reflects the history of the modern working-class movement since 1848. At present it is doubtless the most widely circulated, the most international product of all Socialist literature, the common programme of many millions of workers of all countries, from Siberia to California.

Nevertheless, when it appeared we could not have called it a *Socialist* Manifesto. In 1847 two kinds of people were considered Socialists. On the one hand were the adherents of the various Utopian systems, notably the Owenites in England and the Fourierists in France, both of whom at that date had already dwindled to mere sects gradually dying out. On the other, the manifold types of social quacks who wanted to eliminate social abuses through their various universal panaceas and all kinds of patchwork, without hurting capital and profit in the least. In both cases, people who stood outside the labour movement and who looked for support rather to the 'educated' classes. The section of the working class, however, which demanded a radical reconstruction of society, convinced that mere political revolutions were not enough, then called itself *Communist*. It was still a rough-hewn, only instinctive, and frequently somewhat crude Communism. Yet it was powerful enough to bring into being two systems of Utopian Communism – in France the 'Icarian' Communism of Cabet, and in Germany that of Weitling. Socialism in 1847 signified a bourgeois movement, Communism, a working-class movement. Socialism was, on the Continent at least, quite respectable, whereas Communism was the very opposite. And since we were very decidedly of the opinion as early as then that 'the emancipation of the workers must be the act of the working class itself', we could have no hesitation as to which of the two names we should choose. Nor has it ever occurred to us since to repudiate it.

'Working men of all countries, unite!' But few voices responded when we proclaimed these words to the world forty-two years ago, on the eve of the first Paris Revolution in which the proletariat came out with demands of its own. On 28 September 1864, however, the proletarians of most of the Western European countries joined hands in the International Working Men's Association of glorious memory. True, the International itself lived only nine years. But that the eternal union of the proletarians of all countries created by it is still alive and lives stronger than ever, there is no better witness than this day. Because today, as I write these lines, the European and American proletariat is reviewing its fighting forces, mobilised for the first time, mobilised as *one* army, under *one* flag, for *one* immediate aim: the standard eight-hour working day, to be established by legal enactment, as proclaimed by the Geneva Congress of the International in 1866, and again by the Paris Workers' Congress in 1889.[6] And today's spectacle will open the eyes of the capitalists and landlords of all countries to the fact that today the working men of all countries are united indeed.

If only Marx were still by my side to see this with his own eyes!

London, 1 May 1890   F. ENGELS

Preface to the
Polish Edition of 1892*

THE fact that a new Polish edition of the Communist Manifesto has become necessary gives rise to various thoughts.

First of all, it is noteworthy that of late the Manifesto has become an index, as it were, on the development of large-scale industry on the European continent. In proportion as large-scale industry expands in a given country, the demand grows among the workers of that country for enlightenment regarding their position as the working class in relation to the possessing classes, the socialist movement spreads among them and the demand for the Manifesto increases. Thus, not only the state of the labour movement but also the degree of development of large-scale industry can be measured with fair accuracy in every country by the number of copies of the Manifesto circulated in the language of that country.

Accordingly, the new Polish edition indicates a decided progress of Polish industry. And there can be no doubt whatever that this progress since the previous edition published ten years ago has actually taken place. Russian Poland, Congress Poland, has become the big industrial region of the Russian Empire. Whereas Russian large-scale industry is scattered sporadically – a part round the Gulf of Finland, another in the centre (Moscow and Vladimir), a third along the coasts of the Black and Azov seas, and still others elsewhere – Polish industry has been packed into a relatively small area and enjoys both the advantages and the disadvantages arising from such concentration. The competing Russian manufacturers acknowledged the advan-

*The translation of the Preface to the Polish edition given here is from the German original.

tages when they demanded protective tariffs against Poland, in spite of their ardent desire to transform the Poles into Russians. The disadvantages – for the Polish manufacturers and the Russian government – are manifest in the rapid spread of socialist ideas among the Polish workers and in the growing demand for the Manifesto.

But the rapid development of Polish industry, outstripping that of Russia, is in its turn a new proof of the inexhaustible vitality of the Polish people and a new guarantee of its impending national restoration. And the restoration of an independent strong Poland is a matter which concerns not only the Poles but all of us. A sincere international collaboration of the European nations is possible only if each of these nations is fully autonomous in its own house. The Revolution of 1848, which under the banner of the proletariat, after all, merely let the proletarian fighters do the work of the bourgeoisie, also secured the independence of Italy, Germany, and Hungary through its testamentary executors, Louis Bonaparte and Bismarck; but Poland, which since 1792 had done more for the Revolution than all these three together, was left to its own resources when it succumbed in 1863 to a tenfold greater Russian force. The nobility could neither maintain nor regain Polish independence; today, to the bourgeoisie, this independence is, to say the least, immaterial. Nevertheless, it is a necessity for the harmonious collaboration of the European nations. It can be gained only by the young Polish proletariat, and in its hands it is secure. For the workers of all the rest of Europe need the independence of Poland just as much as the Polish workers themselves.

London, 10 February 1892   F. ENGELS

Preface to the
Italian Edition of 1893

PUBLICATION of the *Manifesto of the Communist Party*
coincided, one may say, with 18 March 1848, the day of the
revolutions in Milan and Berlin, which were armed up-
risings of the two nations situated in the centre, the one,
of the continent of Europe, the other, of the Mediterranean;
two nations until then enfeebled by division and internal
strife, and thus fallen under foreign domination. While Italy
was subject to the Emperor of Austria, Germany under-
went the yoke, not less effective though more indirect, of
the Tsar of all the Russias. The consequences of 18 March
1848 freed both Italy and Germany from this disgrace; if
from 1848 to 1871 these two great nations were reconstituted
and somehow again put on their own, it was, as Karl Marx
used to say, because the men who suppressed the Revolution
of 1848 were, nevertheless, its testamentary executors in
spite of themselves.

Everywhere that revolution was the work of the working
class; it was the latter that built the barricades and paid with
its lifeblood. Only the Paris workers, in overthrowing the
government, had the very definite intention of overthrowing
the bourgeois regime. But conscious though they were of
the fatal antagonism existing between their own class and
the bourgeoisie, still, neither the economic progress of the
country nor the intellectual development of the mass of
French workers had as yet reached the stage which would
have made a social reconstruction possible. In the final
analysis, therefore, the fruits of the revolution were reaped

by the capitalist class. In the other countries, in Italy, in Germany, in Austria, the workers, from the very outset, did nothing but raise the bourgeoisie to power. But in any country the rule of the bourgeoisie is impossible without national independence. Therefore, the Revolution of 1848 had to bring in its train the unity and autonomy of the nations that had lacked them up to then: Italy, Germany, Hungary, Poland will follow in turn.

Thus, if the Revolution of 1848 was not a socialist revolution, it paved the way, prepared the ground for the latter. Through the impetus given to large-scale industry in all countries, the bourgeois regime during the last forty-five years has everywhere created a numerous, concentrated and powerful proletariat. It has thus raised, to use the language of the Manifesto, its own gravediggers. Without restoring autonomy and unity to each nation, it will be impossible to achieve the international union of the proletariat, or the peaceful and intelligent cooperation of these nations towards common aims. Just imagine joint international action by the Italian, Hungarian, German, Polish and Russian workers under the political conditions preceding 1848!

The battles fought in 1848 were thus not fought in vain. Nor have the forty-five years separating us from that revolutionary epoch passed to no purpose. The fruits are ripening, and all I wish is that the publication of this Italian translation may augur as well for the victory of the Italian proletariat as the publication of the original did for the international revolution

The Manifesto does full justice to the revolutionary part played by capitalism in the past. The first capitalist nation was Italy. The close of the feudal Middle Ages, and the opening of the modern capitalist era are marked by a colossal figure: an Italian, Dante, both the last poet of the Middle Ages and the first poet of modern times.

Today, as in 1300, a new historical era is approaching. Will Italy give us the new Dante, who will mark the hour of birth of this new, proletarian era?

London, 1 February 1893   F. ENGELS

MANIFESTO OF
THE COMMUNIST PARTY

A spectre is haunting Europe – the spectre of Communism. All the Powers of old Europe have entered into a holy alliance to exorcize this spectre: Pope and Czar, Metternich and Guizot, French Radicals and German police spies.[7]

Where is the party in opposition that has not been decried as Communistic by its opponents in power? Where the Opposition that has not hurled back the branding reproach of Communism, against the more advanced opposition parties, as well as against its reactionary adversaries?

Two things result from this fact:

I. Communism is already acknowledged by all European Powers to be itself a Power.

II. It is high time that Communists should openly, in the face of the whole world, publish their views, their aims, their tendencies, and meet this nursery tale of the Spectre of Communism with a Manifesto of the party itself.

To this end, Communists of various nationalities have assembled in London, and sketched the following Manifesto, to be published in the English, French, German, Italian, Flemish and Danish languages.

1
Bourgeois and Proletarians*

THE history of all hitherto existing society† is the history of class struggles.

Freeman and slave, patrician and plebeian, lord and serf, guild-master‡ and journeyman, in a word, oppressor and oppressed, stood in constant opposition to one another, carried on an uninterrupted, now hidden, now open fight, a fight that each time ended, either in a revolutionary reconstitution of society at large, or in the common ruin of the contending classes.

*By bourgeoisie is meant the class of modern Capitalists, owners of the means of social production and employers of wage labour. By proletariat, the class of modern wage-labourers who, having no means of production of their own, are reduced to selling their labour power in order to live. [*Note by Engels to the English edition of 1888.*]

†That is, all *written* history. In 1847, the pre-history of society, the social organization existing previous to recorded history, was all but unknown. Since then, Haxthausen discovered common ownership of land in Russia, Maurer proved it to be the social foundation from which all Teutonic races started in history, and by and by village communities were found to be, or to have been the primitive form of society everywhere from India to Ireland. The inner organization of this primitive Communistic society was laid bare, in its typical form, by Morgan's crowning discovery of the true nature of the *gens* and its relation to the *tribe*. With the dissolution of these primeval communities society begins to be differentiated into separate and finally antagonistic classes. I have attempted to retrace this process of dissolution in: *Der Ursprung der Familie, des Privateigenthums und des Staats (The Origin of the Family, Private Property and the State)*, 2nd edition, Stuttgart 1886. [*Note by Engels to the English edition of 1888.*]

‡Guild-master, that is, a full member of a guild, a master within, not a head of a guild. [*Note by Engels to the English edition of 1888.*]

In the earlier epochs of history, we find almost everywhere a complicated arrangement of society into various orders, a manifold gradation of social rank. In ancient Rome we have patricians, knights, plebeians, slaves; in the Middle Ages, feudal lords, vassals, guild-masters, journeymen, apprentices, serfs; in almost all of these classes, again, subordinate gradations.

The modern bourgeois society that has sprouted from the ruins of feudal society has not done away with class antagonisms. It has but established new classes, new conditions of oppression, new forms of struggle in place of the old ones.

Our epoch, the epoch of the bourgeoisie, possesses, however, this distinctive feature: it has simplified the class antagonisms. Society as a whole is more and more splitting up into two great hostile camps, into two great classes directly facing each other: Bourgeoisie and Proletariat.

From the serfs of the Middle Ages sprang the chartered burghers of the earliest towns. From these burgesses the first elements of the bourgeoisie were developed.

The discovery of America, the rounding of the Cape, opened up fresh ground for the rising bourgeoisie. The East-Indian and Chinese markets, the colonization of America, trade with the colonies, the increase in the means of exchange and in commodities generally, gave to commerce, to navigation, to industry, an impulse never before known, and thereby, to the revolutionary element in the tottering feudal society, a rapid development.

The feudal system of industry, under which industrial production was monopolized by closed guilds, now no longer sufficed for the growing wants of the new markets. The manufacturing system took its place. The guild-masters were pushed on one side by the manufacturing middle class; division of labour between the different corporate guilds vanished in the face of division of labour in each single workshop.

Meantime the markets kept ever growing, the demand ever rising. Even manufacture no longer sufficed. Thereupon, steam and machinery revolutionized industrial production. The place of manufacture was taken by the giant, Modern Industry, the place of the industrial middle class, by industrial millionaires, the leaders of whole industrial armies, the modern bourgeois.

Modern industry has established the world market, for which the discovery of America paved the way. This market has given an immense development to commerce, to navigation, to communication by land. This development has, in its turn, reacted on the extension of industry; and in proportion as industry, commerce, navigation, railways extended, in the same proportion the bourgeoisie developed, increased its capital, and pushed into the background every class handed down from the Middle Ages.

We see, therefore, how the modern bourgeoisie is itself the product of a long course of development, of a series of revolutions in the modes of production and of exchange.

Each step in the development of the bourgeoisie was accompanied by a corresponding political advance of that class. An oppressed class under the sway of the feudal nobility, an armed and self-governing association in the medieval commune;* here independent urban republic (as in Italy and Germany), there taxable 'third estate' of the

---

*'Commune' was the name taken, in France, by the nascent towns even before they had conquered from their feudal lords and masters local self-government and political rights as the 'Third Estate'. Generally speaking, for the economical development of the bourgeoisie, England is here taken as the typical country; for its political development, France. [*Note by Engels to the English edition of 1888.*]

This was the name given their urban communities by the townsmen of Italy and France, after they had purchased or wrested their initial rights of self-government from their feudal lords. [*Note by Engels to the German edition of 1890.*]

monarchy (as in France), afterwards, in the period of manufacture proper, serving either the semi-feudal or the absolute monarchy as a counterpoise against the nobility, and, in fact, corner-stone of the great monarchies in general, the bourgeoisie has at last, since the establishment of Modern Industry and of the world market, conquered for itself, in the modern representative State, exclusive political sway. The executive of the modern State is but a committee for managing the common affairs of the whole bourgeoisie.

The bourgeoisie, historically, has played a most revolutionary part.

The bourgeoisie, wherever it has got the upper hand, has put an end to all feudal, patriarchal, idyllic relations. It has pitilessly torn asunder the motley feudal ties that bound man to his 'natural superiors', and has left remaining no other nexus between man and man than naked self-interest, than callous 'cash payment'. It has drowned the most heavenly ecstasies of religious fervour, of chivalrous enthusiasm, of philistine sentimentalism, in the icy water of egotistical calculation. It has resolved personal worth into exchange value, and in place of the numberless indefeasible chartered freedoms, has set up that single, unconscionable freedom – Free Trade. In one word, for exploitation, veiled by religious and political illusions, it has substituted naked, shameless, direct, brutal exploitation.

The bourgeoisie has stripped of its halo every occupation hitherto honoured and looked up to with reverent awe. It has converted the physician, the lawyer, the priest, the poet, the man of science, into its paid wage-labourers.

The bourgeoisie has torn away from the family its sentimental veil, and has reduced the family relation to a mere money relation.

The bourgeoisie has disclosed how it came to pass that the brutal display of vigour in the Middle Ages, which Reactionists so much admire, found its fitting complement in the most slothful indolence. It has been the first to show what man's activity can bring about. It has accomplished wonders far surpassing Egyptian pyramids, Roman aqueducts, and Gothic cathedrals; it has conducted expeditions that put in the shade all former Exoduses of nations and crusades.

The bourgeoisie cannot exist without constantly revolutionizing the instruments of production, and thereby the relations of production, and with them the whole relations of society. Conservation of the old modes of production in unaltered form, was, on the contrary, the first condition of existence for all earlier industrial classes. Constant revolutionizing of production, uninterrupted disturbance of all social conditions, everlasting uncertainty and agitation distinguish the bourgeois epoch from all earlier ones. All fixed, fast-frozen relations, with their train of ancient and venerable prejudices and opinions are swept away, all newformed ones become antiquated before they can ossify. All that is solid melts into air, all that is holy is profaned, and man is at last compelled to face with sober senses, his real conditions of life, and his relations with his kind.

The need of a constantly expanding market for its products chases the bourgeoisie over the whole surface of the globe. It must nestle everywhere, settle everywhere, establish connexions everywhere.

The bourgeoisie has through its exploitation of the world market given a cosmopolitan character to production and consumption in every country. To the great chagrin of Reactionists, it has drawn from under the feet of industry the national ground on which it stood. All old-established national industries have been destroyed or are daily being destroyed. They are dislodged by new industries, whose introduction becomes a life and death question for all civilized nations, by industries that no longer work up indigenous raw material, but raw material drawn from the remotest zones; industries whose products are consumed, not only at home, but in every quarter of the globe. In place of the old wants, satisfied by the productions of the country, we find new wants, requiring for their satisfaction the products of distant lands and climes. In place of the old local and national seclusion and self-sufficiency, we have intercourse in every direction, universal inter-dependence of nations. And as in material, so also in intellectual production. The intellectual creations of individual nations become common property. National one-sidedness and narrow-mindedness become more and more impossible, and from the numerous national and local literatures, there arises a world literature.

The bourgeoisie, by the rapid improvement of all instruments of production, by the immensely facilitated means of communication, draws all, even the most barbarian, nations into civilization. The cheap prices of its commodities are the heavy artillery with which it batters down all Chinese walls, with which it forces the barbarians' intensely obstinate hatred of foreigners to capitulate. It compels all nations, on pain of extinction, to adopt the bourgeois mode of production; it compels them to introduce what it calls civilization into their midst, i.e., to become bourgeois themselves. In one word, it creates a world after its own image.

The bourgeoisie has subjected the country to the rule of the towns. It has created enormous cities, has greatly increased the urban population as compared with the rural, and has thus rescued a considerable part of the population from the idiocy of rural life. Just as it has made the country dependent on the towns, so it has made barbarian and semi-barbarian countries dependent on the civilized ones, nations of peasants on nations of bourgeois, the East on the West.

The bourgeoisie keeps more and more doing away with the scattered state of the population, of the means of production, and of property. It has agglomerated population, centralized means of production, and has concentrated property in a few hands. The necessary consequence of this was political centralization. Independent, or but loosely connected, provinces with separate interests, laws, governments and systems of taxation, became lumped together into one nation, with one government, one code of laws, one national class-interest, one frontier and one customs-tariff.

The bourgeoisie, during its rule of scarce one hundred years, has created more massive and more colossal productive forces than have all preceding generations together. Subjection of Nature's forces to man, machinery, application of chemistry to industry and agriculture, steam-navigation, railways, electric telegraphs, clearing of whole continents for cultivation, canalization of rivers, whole populations conjured out of the ground – what earlier century had even a presentiment that such productive forces slumbered in the lap of social labour?

We see then: the means of production and of exchange, on whose foundation the bourgeoisie built itself up, were generated in feudal society. At a certain stage in the development of these means of production and of exchange, the conditions under which feudal society produced and exchanged, the feudal organization of agriculture and manufacturing industry, in one word, the feudal relations of property became no longer compatible with the already developed productive forces; they became so many fetters. They had to be burst asunder; they were burst asunder.

Into their place stepped free competition, accompanied by a social and political constitution adapted to it, and by the economical and political sway of the bourgeois class.

A similar movement is going on before our own eyes. Modern bourgeois society with its relations of production, of exchange and of property, a society that has conjured up such gigantic means of production and of exchange, is like the sorcerer, who is no longer able to control the powers of the nether world whom he has called up by his spells. For many a decade past the history of industry and commerce is but the history of the revolt of modern productive forces against modern conditions of production, against the property relations that are the conditions for the existence of the bourgeoisie and of its rule. It is enough to mention the commercial crises that by their periodical return put on its trial, each time more threateningly, the existence of the entire bourgeois society. In these crises a great part not only of the existing products, but also of the previously created productive forces, are periodically destroyed. In these crises there breaks out an epidemic that, in all earlier epochs, would have seemed an absurdity – the epidemic of over-production. Society suddenly finds itself put back into a state of momentary barbarism; it appears as if a famine, a universal war of devastation had cut off the supply of every means of subsistence; industry and commerce seem to be destroyed; and why? Because there is too much civilization, too much means of subsistence, too much industry, too much commerce. The productive forces at the disposal of society no longer tend to further the development of the conditions of bourgeois property; on the contrary, they have become too powerful for these conditions, by which they are fettered, and so soon as they overcome these fetters, they bring disorder into the whole of bourgeois society, endanger the existence of bourgeois property. The conditions of bourgeois society are too narrow to comprise the wealth created by them. And how does the bourgeoisie get over these crises? On the one hand by enforced destruction of a mass of productive forces; on the other, by the conquest of new markets, and by the more thorough exploitation of the old ones. That is to say, by paving the way for more extensive and more destructive crises, and by diminishing the means whereby crises are prevented.

The weapons with which the bourgeoisie felled feudalism to the ground are now turned against the bourgeoisie itself.

But not only has the bourgeoisie forged the weapons that bring death to itself; it has also called into existence the men who are to wield those weapons – the modern working class – the proletarians.

In proportion as the bourgeoisie, i.e., capital, is developed, in the same proportion is the proletariat, the modern working class, developed – a class of labourers, who live only so long as they find work, and who find work only so long as their labour increases capital. These labourers, who must sell themselves piecemeal, are a commodity, like every other article of commerce, and are consequently exposed to all the vicissitudes of competition, to all the fluctuations of the market.

Owing to the extensive use of machinery and to division of labour, the work of the proletarians has lost all individual character, and, consequently, all charm for the workman. He becomes an appendage of the machine, and it is only the most simple, most monotonous, and most easily acquired knack, that is required of him. Hence, the cost of production of a workman is restricted, almost entirely, to the means of subsistence that he requires for his maintenance, and for the propagation of his race. But the price of a commodity, and therefore also of labour, is equal to its cost of production. In proportion, therefore, as the repulsiveness of the work increases, the wage decreases. Nay more, in proportion as the use of machinery and division of labour increases, in the same proportion the burden of toil also increases, whether by prolongation of the working hours, by increase of the work exacted in a given time or by increased speed of the machinery, etc.

Modern industry has converted the little workshop of the patriarchal master into the great factory of the industrial capitalist. Masses of labourers, crowded into the factory, are organized like soldiers. As privates of the industrial army they are placed under the command of a perfect hierarchy of officers and sergeants. Not only are they slaves of the bourgeois class, and of the bourgeois State; they are daily and hourly enslaved by the machine, by the overlooker, and, above all, by the individual bourgeois manufacturer himself. The more openly this despotism proclaims gain to be its end and aim, the more petty, the more hateful and the more embittering it is.

The less the skill and exertion of strength implied in manual labour, in other words, the more modern industry becomes developed, the more is the labour of men superseded by that of women. Differences of age and sex have no longer any distinctive social validity for the working class. All are instruments of labour, more or less expensive to use, according to their age and sex.

No sooner is the exploitation of the labourer by the manufacturer, so far, at an end, that he receives his wages in cash, than he is set upon by the other portions of the bourgeoisie, the landlord, the shopkeeper, the pawnbroker, etc.

The lower strata of the middle class – the small tradespeople, shopkeepers, and retired tradesmen generally, the handicraftsmen and peasants – all these sink gradually into the proletariat, partly because their diminutive capital does not suffice for the scale on which Modern Industry is carried on, and is swamped in the competition with the large capitalists, partly because their specialized skill is rendered worthless by new methods of production. Thus the proletariat is recruited from all classes of the population.

The proletariat goes through various stages of development. With its birth begins its struggle with the bourgeoisie. At first the contest is carried on by individual labourers, then by the work-people of a factory, then by the operatives of one trade, in one locality, against the individual bourgeois who directly exploits them. They direct their attacks not against the bourgeois conditions of production, but against the instruments of production themselves; they destroy imported wares that compete with their labour, they smash to pieces machinery, they set factories ablaze, they seek to restore by force the vanished status of the workman of the Middle Ages.

At this stage the labourers still form an incoherent mass scattered over the whole country, and broken up by their mutual competition. If anywhere they unite to form more compact bodies, this is not yet the consequence of their own active union, but of the union of the bourgeoisie, which class, in order to attain its own political ends, is compelled to set the whole proletariat in motion, and is moreover yet, for a time, able to do so. At this stage, therefore, the proletarians do not fight their enemies, but the enemies of their enemies, the remnants of absolute monarchy, the landowners, the non-industrial bourgeois, the petty bourgeoisie. Thus the whole historical movement is concentrated in the hands of the bourgeoisie; every victory so obtained is a victory for the bourgeoisie.

But with the development of industry the proletariat not only increases in number; it becomes concentrated in greater masses, its strength grows, and it feels that strength more. The various interests and conditions of life within the ranks of the proletariat are more and more equalized, in proportion as machinery obliterates all distinctions of labour, and nearly everywhere reduces wages to the same low level. The growing competition among the bourgeois, and the resulting commercial crises, make the wages of the workers ever more fluctuating. The unceasing improvement of machinery, ever more rapidly developing, makes their livelihood more and more precarious; the collisions between individual workmen and individual bourgeois take more and more the character of collisions between two classes. Thereupon the workers begin to form combinations (Trades Unions) against the bourgeois; they club together in order to keep up the rate of wages; they found permanent associations in order to make provision beforehand for these occasional revolts. Here and there the contest breaks out into riots.

Now and then the workers are victorious, but only for a time. The real fruit of their battles lies, not in the immediate result, but in the ever-expanding union of the workers. This union is helped on by the improved means of communication that are created by modern industry and that place the workers of different localities in contact with one another. It was just this contact that was needed to centralize the numerous local struggles, all of the same character, into one national struggle between classes. But every class struggle is a political struggle. And that union, to attain which the burghers of the Middle Ages, with their miserable highways, required centuries, the modern proletarians, thanks to railways, achieve in a few years.

This organization of the proletarians into a class, and consequently into a political party, is continually being upset again by the competition between the workers themselves. But it ever rises up again, stronger, firmer, mightier. It compels legislative recognition of particular interests of the workers, by taking advantage of the divisions among the bourgeoisie itself. Thus the Ten Hours bill in England was carried.

Altogether collisions between the classes of the old society further, in many ways, the course of development of the proletariat. The bourgeoisie finds itself involved in a constant battle. At first with the aristocracy; later on, with those portions of the bourgeoisie itself, whose interests have become antagonistic to the progress of industry; at all times, with the bourgeoisie of foreign countries. In all these battles it sees itself compelled to appeal to the proletariat, to ask for its help, and thus, to drag it into the political arena. The bourgeoisie itself, therefore, supplies the proletariat with its own elements of political and general education, in other words, it furnishes the proletariat with weapons for fighting the bourgeoisie.

Further, as we have already seen, entire sections of the ruling classes are, by the advance of industry, precipitated into the proletariat, or are at least threatened in their conditions of existence. These also supply the proletariat with fresh elements of enlightenment and progress.

Finally, in times when the class struggle nears the decisive hour, the process of dissolution going on within the ruling class, in fact within the whole range of old society, assumes such a violent, glaring character, that a small section of the ruling class cuts itself adrift, and joins the revolutionary class, the class that holds the future in its hands. Just as, therefore, at an earlier period, a section of the nobility went over to the bourgeoisie, so now a portion of the bourgeoisie goes over to the proletariat, and in particular, a portion of the bourgeois ideologists, who have raised themselves to the level of comprehending theoretically the historical movement as a whole.

Of all the classes that stand face to face with the bourgeoisie today, the proletariat alone is a really revolutionary class. The other classes decay and finally disappear in the face of modern industry; the proletariat is its special and essential product.

The lower middle class, the small manufacturer, the shopkeeper, the artisan, the peasant, all these fight against the bourgeoisie, to save from extinction their existence as fractions of the middle class. They are therefore not revolutionary, but conservative. Nay more, they are reactionary, for they try to roll back the wheel of history. If by chance they are revolutionary, they are so only in view of their impending transfer into the proletariat, they thus defend not their present, but their future interests, they desert their own standpoint to place themselves at that of the proletariat.

The 'dangerous class', the social scum, that passively rotting mass thrown off by the lowest layers of old society, may, here and there, be swept into the movement by a proletarian revolution; its conditions of life, however, prepare it far more for the part of a bribed tool of reactionary intrigue.

In the conditions of the proletariat, those of old society at large are already virtually swamped. The proletarian is without property; his relation to his wife and children has no longer anything in common with the bourgeois family relations; modern industrial labour, modern subjection to capital, the same in England as in France, in America as in Germany, has stripped him of every trace of national character. Law, morality, religion, are to him so many bourgeois prejudices, behind which lurk in ambush just as many bourgeois interests.

All the preceding classes that got the upper hand sought to fortify their already acquired status by subjecting society at large to their conditions of appropriation. The proletarians cannot become masters of the productive forces of society, except by abolishing their own previous mode of appropriation, and thereby also every other previous mode of appropriation. They have nothing of their own to secure and to fortify; their mission is to destroy all previous securities for, and insurances of, individual property.

All previous historical movements were movements of minorities, or in the interest of minorities. The proletarian movement is the self-conscious, independent movement of the immense majority, in the interest of the immense majority. The proletariat, the lowest stratum of our present society, cannot stir, cannot raise itself up, without the whole superincumbent strata of official society being sprung into the air.

Though not in substance, yet in form, the struggle of the proletariat with the bourgeoisie is at first a national struggle.

The proletariat of each country must, of course, first of all settle matters with its own bourgeoisie.

In depicting the most general phases of the development of the proletariat, we traced the more or less veiled civil war, raging within existing society, up to the point where that war breaks out into open revolution, and where the violent overthrow of the bourgeoisie lays the foundation for the sway of the proletariat.

Hitherto, every form of society has been based, as we have already seen, on the antagonism of oppressing and oppressed classes. But in order to oppress a class, certain conditions must be assured to it under which it can, at least, continue its slavish existence. The serf, in the period of serfdom, raised himself to membership in the commune, just as the petty bourgeois, under the yoke of feudal absolutism, managed to develop into a bourgeois. The modern labourer, on the contrary, instead of rising with the progress of industry, sinks deeper and deeper below the conditions of existence of his own class. He becomes a pauper, and pauperism develops more rapidly than population and wealth. And here it becomes evident, that the bourgeoisie is unfit any longer to be the ruling class in society, and to impose its conditions of existence upon society as an overriding law. It is unfit to rule because it is incompetent to assure an existence to its slave within his slavery, because it cannot help letting him sink into such a state, that it has to feed him, instead of being fed by him. Society can no longer live under this bourgeoisie, in other words, its existence is no longer compatible with society.

The essential condition for the existence, and for the sway of the bourgeois class, is the formation and augmentation of capital; the condition for capital is wage labour. Wage labour rests exclusively on competition between the labourers. The advance of industry, whose involuntary promoter is the bourgeoisie, replaces the isolation of the labourers, due to competition, by their revolutionary combination, due to association. The development of Modern Industry, therefore, cuts from under its feet the very foundation on which the bourgeoisie produces and appropriates products. What the bourgeoisie, therefore, produces, above all, is its own grave-diggers. Its fall and the victory of the proletariat are equally inevitable.

2
Proletarians and Communists

IN what relation do the Communists stand to the proletarians as a whole?

The Communists do not form a separate party opposed to other working-class parties.

They have no interests separate and apart from those of the proletariat as a whole.

They do not set up any sectarian principles of their own, by which to shape and mould the proletarian movement.

The Communists are distinguished from the other working-class parties by this only: 1. In the national struggles of the proletarians of the different countries, they point out and bring to the front the common interests of the entire proletariat, independently of all nationality. 2. In the various stages of development which the struggle of the working class against the bourgeoisie has to pass through, they always and everywhere represent the interests of the movement as a whole.

The Communists, therefore, are on the one hand, practically, the most advanced and resolute section of the working-class parties of every country, that section which pushes forward all others; on the other hand, theoretically, they have over the great mass of the proletariat the advantage of clearly understanding the line of march, the conditions, and the ultimate general results of the proletarian movement.

The immediate aim of the Communists is the same as that of all the other proletarian parties: formation of the proletariat into a class, overthrow of the bourgeois supremacy, conquest of political power by the proletariat.

The theoretical conclusions of the Communists are in no way based on ideas or principles that have been invented, or discovered, by this or that would-be universal reformer.

They merely express, in general terms, actual relations springing from an existing class struggle, from a historical movement going on under our very eyes. The abolition of existing property relations is not at all a distinctive feature of Communism.

All property relations in the past have continually been subject to historical change consequent upon the change in historical conditions.

The French Revolution, for example, abolished feudal property in favour of bourgeois property.

The distinguishing feature of Communism is not the abolition of property generally, but the abolition of bourgeois property. But modern bourgeois private property is the final and most complete expression of the system of producing and appropriating products, that is based on class antagonisms, on the exploitation of the many by the few.

In this sense, the theory of the Communists may be summed up in the single sentence: Abolition of private property.

We Communists have been reproached with the desire of abolishing the right of personally acquiring property as the fruit of a man's own labour, which property is alleged to be the ground work of all personal freedom, activity and independence.

Hard-won, self-acquired, self-earned property! Do you mean the property of the petty artisan and of the small peasant, a form of property that preceded the bourgeois form? There is no need to abolish that; the development of industry has to a great extent already destroyed it, and is still destroying it daily.

Or do you mean modern bourgeois private property?

But does wage labour create any property for the labourer? Not a bit. It creates capital, i.e., that kind of property which exploits wage labour, and which cannot increase except upon condition of begetting a new supply of wage labour for fresh exploitation. Property, in its present form, is based on the antagonism of capital and wage labour. Let us examine both sides of this antagonism.

To be a capitalist is to have not only a purely personal but a social *status* in production. Capital is a collective product, and only by the united action of many members, nay, in the last resort, only by the united action of all members of society, can it be set in motion.

Capital is, therefore, not a personal, it is a social power.

When, therefore, capital is converted into common property, into the property of all members of society, personal property is not thereby transformed into social property. It is only the social character of the property that is changed. It loses its class character.

Let us now take wage labour.

The average price of wage labour is the minimum wage, i.e., that quantum of the means of subsistence which is absolutely requisite to keep the labourer in bare existence as a labourer. What, therefore, the wage-labourer appropriates by means of his labour, merely suffices to prolong and reproduce a bare existence. We by no means intend to abolish this personal appropriation of the products of labour, an appropriation that is made for the maintenance and reproduction of human life, and that leaves no surplus wherewith to command the labour of others. All that we want to do away with is the miserable character of this appropriation, under which the labourer lives merely to increase capital, and is allowed to live only in so far as the interest of the ruling class requires it.

In bourgeois society, living labour is but a means to increase accumulated labour. In Communist society, accumulated labour is but a means to widen, to enrich, to promote the existence of the labourer.

In bourgeois society, therefore, the past dominates the

present; in Communist society, the present dominates the past. In bourgeois society capital is independent and has individuality, while the living person is dependent and has no individuality.

And the abolition of this state of things is called by the bourgeois, abolition of individuality and freedom! And rightly so. The abolition of bourgeois individuality, bourgeois independence, and bourgeois freedom is undoubtedly aimed at.

By freedom is meant, under the present bourgeois conditions of production, free trade, free selling and buying.

But if selling and buying disappears, free selling and buying disappears also. This talk about free selling and buying, and all the other 'brave words' of our bourgeoisie about freedom in general, have a meaning, if any, only in contrast with restricted selling and buying, with the fettered traders of the Middle Ages, but have no meaning when opposed to the Communistic abolition of buying and selling, of the bourgeois conditions of production, and of the bourgeoisie itself.

You are horrified at our intending to do away with private property. But in your existing society, private property is already done away with for nine-tenths of the population; its existence for the few is solely due to its non-existence in the hands of those nine-tenths. You reproach us, therefore, with intending to do away with a form of property the necessary condition for whose existence is the non-existence of any property for the immense majority of society.

In one word, you reproach us with intending to do away with your property. Precisely so; that is just what we intend.

From the moment when labour can no longer be converted into capital, money, or rent, into a social power capable of being monopolized, i.e., from the moment when individual property can no longer be transformed into bourgeois property, into capital, from that moment, you say, individuality vanishes.

You must, therefore, confess that by 'individual' you mean no other person than the bourgeois, than the middle-class owner of property. This person must, indeed, be swept out of the way, and made impossible.

Communism deprives no man of the power to appropriate the products of society; all that it does is to deprive him of the power to subjugate the labour of others by means of such appropriation.

It has been objected that upon the abolition of private property all work will cease, and universal laziness will overtake us.

According to this, bourgeois society ought long ago to have gone to the dogs through sheer idleness; for those of its members who work, acquire nothing, and those who acquire anything, do not work. The whole of this objection is but another expression of the tautology: that there can no longer be any wage labour when there is no longer any capital.

All objections urged against the Communistic mode of producing and appropriating material products, have, in the same way, been urged against the Communistic modes of producing and appropriating intellectual products. Just as, to the bourgeois, the disappearance of class property is the disappearance of production itself, so the disappearance of class culture is to him identical with the disappearance of all culture.

That culture, the loss of which he laments, is, for the enormous majority, a mere training to act as a machine.

But don't wrangle with us so long as you apply, to our intended abolition of bourgeois property, the standard of your bourgeois notions of freedom, culture, law, &c. Your very ideas are but the outgrowth of the conditions of your bourgeois production and bourgeois property, just as your jurisprudence is but the will of your class made into a law for all, a will, whose essential character and direction are determined by the economical conditions of existence of your class.

The selfish misconception that induces you to transform into eternal laws of nature and of reason, the social forms springing from your present mode of production and form of property – historical relations that rise and disappear in the progress of production – this misconception you share with every ruling class that has preceded you. What you see clearly in the case of ancient property, what you admit in the case of feudal property, you are of course forbidden to admit in the case of your own bourgeois form of property.

Abolition of the family! Even the most radical flare up at this infamous proposal of the Communists.

On what foundation is the present family, the bourgeois family, based? On capital, on private gain. In its completely developed form this family exists only among the bourgeoisie. But this state of things finds its complement in the practical absence of the family among the proletarians, and in public prostitution.

The bourgeois family will vanish as a matter of course when its complement vanishes, and both will vanish with the vanishing of capital.

Do you charge us with wanting to stop the exploitation of children by their parents? To this crime we plead guilty.

But, you will say, we destroy the most hallowed of relations, when we replace home education by social.

And your education! Is not that also social, and determined by the social conditions under which you educate, by the intervention, direct or indirect, of society, by means of schools, &c? The Communists have not invented the intervention of society in education; they do but seek to alter the character of that intervention, and to rescue education from the influence of the ruling class.

The bourgeois clap-trap about the family and education, about the hallowed co-relation of parent and child, becomes all the more disgusting, the more, by the action of Modern Industry, all family ties among the proletarians are torn asunder, and their children transformed into simple articles of commerce and instruments of labour.

But you Communists would introduce community of women, screams the whole bourgeoisie in chorus.

The bourgeois sees in his wife a mere instrument of production. He hears that the instruments of production are to be exploited in common, and, naturally, can come to no other conclusion than that the lot of being common to all will likewise fall to the women.

He has not even a suspicion that the real point aimed at is to do away with the status of women as mere instruments of production.

For the rest, nothing is more ridiculous than the virtuous indignation of our bourgeois at the community of women which, they pretend, is to be openly and officially established by the Communists. The Communists have no need to introduce community of women; it has existed almost from time immemorial.

Our bourgeois, not content with having the wives and daughters of their proletarians at their disposal, not to speak of common prostitutes, take the greatest pleasure in seducing each other's wives.

Bourgeois marriage is in reality a system of wives in common and thus, at the most, what the Communists might possibly be reproached with, is that they desire to introduce, in substitution for a hypocritically concealed, an openly legalized community of women. For the rest, it is self-evident that the abolition of the present system of production must bring with it the abolition of the community of women springing from that system, i.e., of prostitution both public and private.

The Communists are further reproached with desiring to abolish countries and nationality.

The working men have no country. We cannot take from them what they have not got. Since the proletariat must first of all acquire political supremacy, must rise to be the leading class of the nation, must constitute itself *the* nation, it is, so far, itself national, though not in the bourgeois sense of the word.

National differences and antagonisms between peoples are daily more and more vanishing, owing to the development of the bourgeoisie, to freedom of commerce, to the world market, to uniformity in the mode of production and in the conditions of life corresponding thereto.

The supremacy of the proletariat will cause them to vanish still faster. United action, of the leading civilized countries at least, is one of the first conditions for the emancipation of the proletariat.

In proportion as the exploitation of one individual by another is put an end to, the exploitation of one nation by another will also be put an end to. In proportion as the antagonism between classes within the nation vanishes, the hostility of one nation to another will come to an end.

The charges against Communism made from a religious, a philosophical, and, generally, from an ideological standpoint, are not deserving of serious examination.

Does it require deep intuition to comprehend that man's ideas, views and conceptions, in one word, man's consciousness, changes with every change in the conditions of his material existence, in his social relations and in his social life?

What else does the history of ideas prove, than that intellectual production changes in character in proportion as material production is changed? The ruling ideas of each age have ever been the ideas of its ruling class.

When people speak of ideas that revolutionize society,

they do but express the fact, that within the old society, the elements of a new one have been created, and that the dissolution of the old ideas keeps even pace with the dissolution of the old conditions of existence.

When the ancient world was in its last throes, the ancient religions were overcome by Christianity. When Christian ideas succumbed in the 18th century to rationalist ideas, feudal society fought its death battle with the then revolutionary bourgeoisie. The ideas of religious liberty and freedom of conscience, merely gave expression to the sway of free competition within the domain of knowledge.

'Undoubtedly,' it will be said, 'religious, moral, philosophical and juridical ideas have been modified in the course of historical development. But religion, morality, philosophy, political science, and law, constantly survived this change.

'There are, besides, eternal truths, such as Freedom, Justice, etc., that are common to all states of society. But Communism abolishes eternal truths, it abolishes all religion, and all morality, instead of constituting them on a new basis; it therefore acts in contradiction to all past historical experience.'

What does this accusation reduce itself to? The history of all past society has consisted in the development of class antagonisms, antagonisms that assumed different forms at different epochs.

But whatever form they may have taken, one fact is common to all past ages, viz., the exploitation of one part of society by the other. No wonder, then, that the social consciousness of past ages, despite all the multiplicity and variety it displays, moves within certain common forms, or general ideas, which cannot completely vanish except with the total disappearance of class antagonisms.

The Communist revolution is the most radical rupture with traditional property relations; no wonder that its development involves the most radical rupture with traditional ideas.

But let us have done with the bourgeois objections to Communism.

We have seen above, that the first step in the revolution by the working class, is to raise the proletariat to the position of ruling class, to win the battle of democracy.

The proletariat will use its political supremacy to wrest, by degrees, all capital from the bourgeoisie, to centralize all instruments of production in the hands of the State, i.e., of the proletariat organized as the ruling class; and to increase the total of productive forces as rapidly as possible.

Of course, in the beginning, this cannot be effected except by means of despotic inroads on the rights of property, and on the conditions of bourgeois production; by means of measures, therefore, which appear economically insufficient and untenable, but which, in the course of the movement, outstrip themselves, necessitate further inroads upon the old social order, and are unavoidable as a means of entirely revolutionizing the mode of production.

These measures will of course be different in different countries.

Nevertheless, in the most advanced countries, the following will be pretty generally applicable:

1. Abolition of property in land and application of all rents of land to public purposes.

2. A heavy progressive or graduated income tax.

3. Abolition of all right of inheritance.

4. Confiscation of the property of all emigrants and rebels.

5. Centralization of credit in the hands of the State, by means of a national bank with State capital and an exclusive monopoly.

6. Centralization of the means of communication and transport in the hands of the State.

7. Extension of factories and instruments of production owned by the State; the bringing into cultivation of wastelands, and the improvement of the soil generally in accordance with a common plan.

8. Equal liability of all to labour. Establishment of industrial armies, especially for agriculture.

9. Combination of agriculture with manufacturing industries; gradual abolition of the distinction between town and country, by a more equable distribution of the population over the country.

10. Free education for all children in public schools. Abolition of children's factory labour in its present form. Combination of education with industrial production, &c., &c.

When, in the course of development, class distinctions have disappeared, and all production has been concentrated in the whole nation, the public power will lose its political character. Political power, properly so called, is merely the organized power of one class for oppressing another. If the proletariat during its contest with the bourgeoisie is compelled, by the force of circumstances, to organize itself as a class, if, by means of a revolution, it makes itself the ruling class, and, as such, sweeps away by force the old conditions of production, then it will, along with these conditions, have swept away the conditions for the existence of class antagonisms and of classes generally, and will thereby have abolished its own supremacy as a class.

In place of the old bourgeois society, with its classes and class antagonisms, we shall have an association, in which the free development of each is the condition for the free development of all.

3
Socialist and Communist Literature

I. REACTIONARY SOCIALISM

a. Feudal Socialism

OWING to their historical position, it became the vocation of the aristocracies of France and England to write pamphlets against modern bourgeois society. In the French revolution of July 1830, and in the English reform agitation, these aristocracies again succumbed to the hateful upstart.[8] Thenceforth, a serious political contest was altogether out of question. A literary battle alone remained possible. But even in the domain of literature the old cries of the restoration period* had become impossible.

In order to arouse sympathy, the aristocracy were obliged to lose sight, apparently, of their own interests, and to formulate their indictment against the bourgeoisie in the interest of the exploited working class alone. Thus the aristocracy took their revenge by singing lampoons on their new master, and whispering in his ears sinister prophecies of coming catastrophe.

In this way arose feudal Socialism: half lamentation, half lampoon; half echo of the past, half menace of the future; at times, by its bitter, witty and incisive criticism, striking the bourgeoisie to the very heart's core; but always ludicrous in its effect, through total incapacity to comprehend the march of modern history.

The aristocracy, in order to rally the people to them, waved the proletarian alms-bag in front for a banner. But

*Not the English Restoration 1660 to 1689, but the French Restoration 1814 to 1830. [Note by Engels to the English edition of 1888.]

the people, so often as it joined them, saw on their hind-quarters the old feudal coats of arms, and deserted with loud and irreverent laughter.

One section of the French Legitimists and 'Young England'⁹ exhibited this spectacle.

In pointing out that their mode of exploitation was different to that of the bourgeoisie, the feudalists forget that they exploited under circumstances and conditions that were quite different, and that are now antiquated. In showing that, under their rule, the modern proletariat never existed, they forget that the modern bourgeoisie is the necessary offspring of their own form of society.

For the rest, so little do they conceal the reactionary character of their criticism that their chief accusation against the bourgeoisie amounts to this, that under the bourgeois *régime* a class is being developed, which is destined to cut up root and branch the old order of society.

What they upbraid the bourgeoisie with is not so much that it creates a proletariat, as that it creates a *revolutionary* proletariat.

In political practice, therefore, they join in all coercive measures against the working class; and in ordinary life, despite their high-falutin phrases, they stoop to pick up the golden apples dropped from the tree of industry, and to barter truth, love, and honour for traffic in wool, beetroot-sugar, and potato spirits.*

As the parson has ever gone hand in hand with the landlord, so has Clerical Socialism with Feudal Socialism.

*This applies chiefly to Germany where the landed aristocracy and squirearchy have large portions of their estates cultivated for their own account by stewards, and are, moreover, extensive beetroot-sugar manufacturers and distillers of potato spirits. The wealthier British aristocracy are, as yet, rather above that; but they, too, know how to make up for declining rents by lending their names to floaters of more or less shady joint-stock companies. [*Note by Engels to the English edition of 1888.*]

Nothing is easier than to give Christian asceticism a Socialist tinge. Has not Christianity declaimed against private property, against marriage, against the State? Has it not preached in the place of these, charity and poverty, celibacy and mortification of the flesh, monastic life and Mother Church? Christian Socialism is but the holy water with which the priest consecrates the heart-burnings of the aristocrat.

b. Petty-Bourgeois Socialism

The feudal aristocracy was not the only class that was ruined by the bourgeoisie, not the only class whose conditions of existence pined and perished in the atmosphere of modern bourgeois society. The medieval burgesses and the small peasant proprietors were the precursors of the modern bourgeoisie. In those countries which are but little developed, industrially and commercially, these two classes still vegetate side by side with the rising bourgeoisie.

In countries where modern civilization has become fully developed, a new class of petty bourgeois has been formed, fluctuating between proletariat and bourgeoisie and ever renewing itself as a supplementary part of bourgeois society. The individual members of this class, however, are being constantly hurled down into the proletariat by the action of competition, and, as modern industry develops, they even see the moment approaching when they will completely disappear as an independent section of modern society, to be replaced, in manufacture, agriculture and commerce, by overlookers, bailiffs and shopmen.

In countries like France, where the peasants constitute far more than half of the population, it was natural that writers who sided with the proletariat against the bourgeoisie, should use, in their criticism of the bourgeois *régime*, the standard of the peasant and petty bourgeois, and from the standpoint of these intermediate classes should take up the cudgels for the working class. Thus arose petty-bourgeois Socialism. Sismondi was the head of this school, not only in France but also in England.[10]

This school of Socialism dissected with great acuteness the contradictions in the conditions of modern production. It laid bare the hypocritical apologies of economists. It proved, incontrovertibly, the disastrous effects of machinery and division of labour; the concentration of capital and land in a few hands; over-production and crises; it pointed out the inevitable ruin of the petty bourgeois and peasant, the misery of the proletariat, the anarchy in production, the crying inequalities in the distribution of wealth, the industrial war of extermination between nations, the dissolution of old moral bonds, of the old family relations, of the old nationalities.

In its positive aims, however, this form of Socialism aspires either to restoring the old means of production and of exchange, and with them the old property relations, and the old society, or to cramping the modern means of production and of exchange, within the framework of the old property relations that have been, and were bound to be, exploded by those means. In either case, it is both reactionary and Utopian.

Its last words are: corporate guilds for manufacture; patriarchal relations in agriculture.

Ultimately, when stubborn historical facts had dispersed all intoxicating effects of self-deception, this form of Socialism ended in a miserable fit of the blues.

c. German, or 'True', Socialism

The Socialist and Communist literature of France, a literature that originated under the pressure of a bourgeoisie in power, and that was the expression of the struggle against this power, was introduced into Germany at a time when the bourgeoisie, in that country, had just begun its contest with feudal absolutism.

German philosophers, would-be philosophers, and *beaux esprits*, eagerly seized on this literature, only forgetting, that when these writings immigrated from France into Germany, French social conditions had not immigrated along with them. In contact with German social conditions, this French literature lost all its immediate practical significance, and assumed a purely literary aspect. Thus, to the German philosophers of the Eighteenth Century, the demands of the first French Revolution were nothing more than the demands of 'Practical Reason' in general, and the utterance of the will of the revolutionary French bourgeoisie signified in their eyes the laws of pure Will, of Will as it was bound to be, of true human Will generally.

The work of the German *literati* consisted solely in bringing the new French ideas into harmony with their ancient philosophical conscience, or rather, in annexing the French ideas without deserting their own philosophic point of view.

This annexation took place in the same way in which a foreign language is appropriated, namely, by translation.

It is well known how the monks wrote silly lives of Catholic Saints *over* the manuscripts on which the classical works of ancient heathendom had been written. The German *literati* reversed this process with the profane French literature. They wrote their philosophical nonsense beneath the French original. For instance, beneath the French criticism of the economic functions of money, they wrote 'Alienation of Humanity', and beneath the French criticism of the bourgeois State they wrote, 'Dethronement of the Category of the General', and so forth.

The introduction of these philosophical phrases at the back of the French historical criticisms they dubbed 'Philosophy of Action', 'True Socialism', 'German Science of Socialism', 'Philosophical Foundation of Socialism', and so on.

The French Socialist and Communist literature was thus completely emasculated. And, since it ceased in the hands of the German to express the struggle of one class with the other, he felt conscious of having overcome 'French one-sidedness' and of representing, not true requirements, but the requirements of Truth; not the interests of the proletariat, but the interests of Human Nature, of Man in general, who belongs to no class, has no reality, who exists only in the misty realm of philosophical fantasy.

This German Socialism, which took its schoolboy task so seriously and solemnly, and extolled its poor stock-in-trade in such mountebank fashion, meanwhile gradually lost its pedantic innocence.

The fight of the German, and, especially of the Prussian bourgeoisie, against feudal aristocracy and absolute monarchy, in other words, the liberal movement, became more earnest.

By this, the long wished-for opportunity was offered to 'True' Socialism of confronting the political movement with the Socialist demands, of hurling the traditional anathemas against liberalism, against representative government, against bourgeois competition, bourgeois freedom of the press, bourgeois legislation, bourgeois liberty and equality, and of preaching to the masses that they had nothing to gain, and everything to lose, by this bourgeois movement. German Socialism forgot, in the nick of time, that the French criticism, whose silly echo it was, presupposed the existence of modern bourgeois society, with its corresponding economic conditions of existence, and the political constitution adapted thereto, the very things whose attainment was the object of the pending struggle in Germany.

To the absolute governments, with their following of

parsons, professors, country squires and officials, it served as a welcome scarecrow against the threatening bourgeoisie.

It was a sweet finish after the bitter pills of floggings and bullets with which these same governments, just at that time, dosed the German working-class risings.

While this 'True' Socialism thus served the governments as a weapon for fighting the German bourgeoisie, it, at the same time, directly represented a reactionary interest, the interest of the German Philistines. In Germany the *petty-bourgeois* class, a relic of the sixteenth century, and since then constantly cropping up again under various forms, is the real social basis of the existing state of things.

To preserve this class is to preserve the existing state of things in Germany. The industrial and political supremacy of the bourgeoisie threatens it with certain destruction; on the one hand, from the concentration of capital; on the other, from the rise of a revolutionary proletariat. 'True' Socialism appeared to kill these two birds with one stone. It spread like an epidemic.

The robe of speculative cobwebs, embroidered with flowers of rhetoric, steeped in the dew of sickly sentiment, this transcendental robe in which the German Socialists wrapped their sorry 'eternal truths', all skin and bone, served to wonderfully increase the sale of their goods amongst such a public.

And on its part, German Socialism recognized, more and more, its own calling as the bombastic representative of the petty-bourgeois Philistine.

It proclaimed the German nation to be the model nation, and the German petty Philistine to be the typical man. To every villainous meanness of this model man it gave a hidden, higher, Socialistic interpretation, the exact contrary of its real character. It went to the extreme length of directly opposing the 'brutally destructive' tendency of Communism, and of proclaiming its supreme and impartial contempt of all class struggles. With very few exceptions, all the so-called Socialist and Communist publications that now (1847) circulate in Germany belong to the domain of this foul and enervating literature.*

II. CONSERVATIVE, OR BOURGEOIS, SOCIALISM

A part of the bourgeoisie is desirous of redressing social grievances, in order to secure the continued existence of bourgeois society.

To this section belong economists, philanthropists, humanitarians, improvers of the condition of the working class, organisers of charity, members of societies for the prevention of cruelty to animals, temperance fanatics, hole-and-corner reformers of every imaginable kind. This form of Socialism has, moreover, been worked out into complete systems.

We may cite Proudhon's *Philosophie de la Misère* as an example of this form.[11]

The Socialistic bourgeois want all the advantages of modern social conditions without the struggles and dangers necessarily resulting therefrom. They desire the existing state of society minus its revolutionary and disintegrating elements. They wish for a bourgeoisie without a proletariat. The bourgeoisie naturally conceives the world in which it is supreme to be the best; and bourgeois Socialism develops this comfortable conception into various more or less complete systems. In requiring the proletariat to carry out such a system, and thereby to march straightway into the social New Jerusalem, it but requires in reality, that the proletariat

*The revolutionary storm of 1848 swept away this whole shabby tendency and cured its protagonists of the desire to dabble further in Socialism. The chief representative and classical type of this tendency is Herr Karl Grün. [*Note by Engels to the German edition of 1890.*]

should remain within the bounds of existing society, but should cast away all its hateful ideas concerning the bourgeoisie.

A second and more practical, but less systematic, form of this Socialism sought to depreciate every revolutionary movement in the eyes of the working class, by showing that no mere political reform, but only a change in the material conditions of existence, in economical relations, could be of any advantage to them. By changes in the material conditions of existence, this form of Socialism, however, by no means understands abolition of the bourgeois relations of production, an abolition that can be effected only by a revolution, but administrative reforms, based on the continued existence of these relations; reforms, therefore, that in no respect affect the relations between capital and labour, but, at the best, lessen the cost, and simplify the administrative work, of bourgeois government.

Bourgeois Socialism attains adequate expression, when, and only when, it becomes a mere figure of speech.

Free trade: for the benefit of the working class. Protective duties: for the benefit of the working class. Prison Reform: for the benefit of the working class. This is the last word and the only seriously meant word of bourgeois Socialism.

It is summed up in the phrase: the bourgeois is a bourgeois – for the benefit of the working class.

III. CRITICAL-UTOPIAN SOCIALISM AND COMMUNISM

We do not here refer to that literature which, in every great modern revolution, has always given voice to the demands of the proletariat, such as the writings of Babeuf and others.[12]

The first direct attempts of the proletariat to attain its own ends, made in times of universal excitement, when feudal society was being overthrown, these attempts necessarily failed, owing to the then undeveloped state of the proletariat, as well as to the absence of the economic conditions for its emancipation, conditions that had yet to be produced, and could be produced by the impending bourgeois epoch alone. The revolutionary literature that accompanied these first movements of the proletariat had necessarily a reactionary character. It inculcated universal asceticism and social levelling in its crudest form.

The Socialist and Communist systems properly so called, those of Saint-Simon, Fourier, Owen and others,[13] spring into existence in the early undeveloped period, described above, of the struggle between proletariat and bourgoisie (see Section I. Bourgeois and Proletarians).

The founders of these systems see, indeed, the class antagonisms, as well as the action of the decomposing elements in the prevailing form of society. But the proletariat, as yet in its infancy, offers to them the spectacle of a class without any historical initiative or any independent political movement.

Since the development of class antagonism keeps even pace with the development of industry, the economic situation, as they find it, does not as yet offer to them the material conditions for the emancipation of the proletariat. They therefore search after a new social science, after new social laws, that are to create these conditions.

Historical action is to yield to their personal inventive action, historically created conditions of emancipation to fantastic ones, and the gradual, spontaneous class organization of the proletariat to an organization of society specially contrived by these inventors. Future history resolves itself, in their eyes, into the propaganda and the practical carrying out of their social plans.

In the formation of their plans they are conscious of

caring chiefly for the interests of the working class, as being the most suffering class. Only from the point of view of being the most suffering class does the proletariat exist for them.

The undeveloped state of the class struggle, as well as their own surroundings, causes Socialists of this kind to consider themselves far superior to all class antagonisms. They want to improve the condition of every member of society, even that of the most favoured. Hence, they habitually appeal to society at large, without distinction of class; nay, by preference, to the ruling class. For how can people, when once they understand their system, fail to see in it the best possible plan of the best possible state of society?

Hence, they reject all political, and especially all revolutionary, action; they wish to attain their ends by peaceful means, and endeavour, by small experiments, necessarily doomed to failure, and by the force of example, to pave the way for the new social Gospel.

Such fantastic pictures of future society, painted at a time when the proletariat is still in a very undeveloped state and has but a fantastic conception of its own position correspond with the first instinctive yearnings of that class for a general reconstruction of society.

But these Socialist and Communist publications contain also a critical element. They attack every principle of existing society. Hence they are full of the most valuable materials for the enlightenment of the working class. The practical measures proposed in them – such as the abolition of the distinction between town and country, of the family, of the carrying on of industries for the account of private individuals, and of the wage system, the proclamation of social harmony, the conversion of the functions of the State into a mere superintendence of production, all these proposals point solely to the disappearance of class antagonisms which were, at that time, only just cropping up, and which, in these publications, are recognized in their earliest indistinct and undefined forms only. These proposals, therefore, are of a purely Utopian character.

The significance of Critical-Utopian Socialism and Communism bears an inverse relation to historical development. In proportion as the modern class struggle develops and takes definite shape, this fantastic standing apart from the contest, these fantastic attacks on it, lose all practical value and all theoretical justification. Therefore, although the originators of these systems were, in many respects, revolutionary, their disciples have, in every case, formed mere reactionary sects. They hold fast by the original views of their masters, in opposition to the progressive historical development of the proletariat. They, therefore, endeavour, and that consistently, to deaden the class struggle and to reconcile the class antagonisms. They still dream of experimental realization of their social Utopias, of founding isolated '*phalanstères*', of establishing 'Home Colonies', of setting up a 'Little Icaria'* – duodecimo editions of the New Jerusalem – and to realize all these castles in the air, they are compelled to appeal to the feelings and purses of the bourgeois. By degrees they sink into the category of the reactionary conservative Socialists depicted above, differing from these only by more systematic pedantry, and by their fanatical and superstitious belief in the miraculous effects of their social science.

They, therefore, violently oppose all political action on

Phalanstères were Socialist colonies on the plan of Charles Fourier; *Icaria* was the name given by Cabet to his Utopia and, later on, to his American Communist colony. [*Note by Engels to the English edition of 1888.*]

'Home colonies' were what Owen called his Communist model societies. *Phalanstères* was the name of the public palaces planned by Fourier. *Icaria* was the name given to the Utopian land of fancy, whose Communist institutions Cabet portrayed. [*Note by Engels to the German edition of 1890.*]

the part of the working class; such action, according to them, can only result from blind unbelief in the new Gospel.

The Owenites in England, and the Fourierists in France, respectively oppose the Chartists and the *Réformistes*.†

†This refers to the adherents of the newspaper *La Réforme*, which was published in Paris from 1843 to 1850.

4

Position of the Communists in Relation to the Various Existing Opposition Parties

SECTION 2 has made clear the relations of the Communists to the existing working-class parties, such as the Chartists in England and the Agrarian Reformers in America.

The Communists fight for the attainment of the immediate aims, for the enforcement of the momentary interests of the working class; but in the movement of the present, they also represent and take care of the future of that movement. In France the Communists ally themselves with the Social-Democrats,* against the conservative and radical bourgeoisie, reserving, however, the right to take up a critical position in regard to phrases and illusions traditionally handed down from the great Revolution.

In Switzerland they support the Radicals, without losing sight of the fact that this party consists of antagonistic elements, partly of Democratic Socialists, in the French sense, partly of radical bourgeois.

In Poland they support the party that insists on an agrarian

---

*The party then represented in Parliament by Ledru-Rollin, in literature by Louis Blanc, in the daily press by the *Réforme*. The name of Social-Democracy signified, with these its inventors, a section of the Democratic or Republican party more or less tinged with Socialism. [*Note by Engels to the English edition of 1888.*]

The party in France which at that time called itself Socialist-Democratic was represented in political life by Ledru-Rollin and in literature by Louis Blanc; thus it differed immeasurably from present-day German Social-Democracy. [*Note by Engels to the German edition of 1890.*]

revolution as the prime condition for national emancipation, that party which fomented the insurrection of Cracow in 1846.

In Germany they fight with the bourgeoisie whenever it acts in a revolutionary way, against the absolute monarchy, the feudal squirearchy, and the petty bourgeoisie.

But they never cease, for a single instant, to instil into the working class the clearest possible recognition of the hostile antagonism between bourgeoisie and proletariat, in order that the German workers may straightway use, as so many weapons against the bourgeoisie, the social and political conditions that the bourgeoisie must necessarily introduce along with its supremacy, and in order that, after the fall of the reactionary classes in Germany, the fight against the bourgeoisie itself may immediately begin.

The Communists turn their attention chiefly to Germany, because that country is on the eve of a bourgeois revolution that is bound to be carried out under more advanced conditions of European civilization, and with a much more developed proletariat, than that of England was in the seventeenth, and of France in the eighteenth century, and because the bourgeois revolution in Germany will be but the prelude to an immediately following proletarian revolution.

In short, the Communists everywhere support every revolutionary movement against the existing social and political order of things.

In all these movements they bring to the front, as the leading question in each, the property question, no matter what its degree of development at the time.

Finally, they labour everywhere for the union and agreement of the democratic parties of all countries.

The Communists disdain to conceal their views and aims. They openly declare that their ends can be attained only by the forcible overthrow of all existing social conditions. Let the ruling classes tremble at a Communistic revolution. The proletarians have nothing to lose but their chains. They have a world to win.

WORKING MEN OF ALL COUNTRIES, UNITE!

Notes by A. J. P. Taylor

1. This sentence omits to say that the Communist League was itself the creation, more or less imaginary, of Marx and Engels.

2. On 24 February 1848, the constitutional monarchy of Louis Philippe was overthrown, and a provisional government set up, which shortly afterwards proclaimed a republic.

3. In June 1848 the masses of Paris were provoked into insurrection by the closing of the National Workshops. The insurrection was crushed by Cavaignac who then became dictator.

4. The Paris Commune held power during April and May 1871. It was mainly a protest against peace with Germany and against the harsh conditions following the Franco-German war.

5. Alexander II was assassinated by social revolutionaries in 1881. Alexander III, his son, sought and found safety in the seclusion of Gatchina.

6. This congress inaugurated the Second International.

7. Metternich, chancellor of the Austrian empire, was overthrown by revolution on 13 March 1848. Guizot, French premier, was overthrown by the February revolution.

8. The French revolution of July 1830 overthrew the legitimist Charles X and raised up the bourgeois monarch Louis Philippe. The English reform act of 1832 gave the vote to substantial householders.

9. 'Young England' was a rather fancy literary movement, led by Disraeli and his aristocratic friends.

10. Sismondi (1773–1842) was a French writer on political economy whom Marx much admired.

11. Proudhon (1809–65) coined two immortal phrases: 'Property is theft' and 'universal suffrage is counter-revolution'. He advocated co-operative societies instead of political revolution and put his faith in Napoleon III. His followers gave Marx trouble during the First International.

12. Babeuf (1760–97) attempted to lead a new proletarian rising towards the end of the great French revolution.

13. Saint-Simon (1760–1825) and Fourier (1772–1837)

123

described socialist Utopias. Robert Owen (1771–1858) preached cooperation and ran a cotton mill on idealistic lines. His followers founded Utopian colonies in the United States. In old age, he became a spiritualist.

READ MORE IN PENGUIN

In every corner of the world, on every subject under the sun, Penguin represents quality and variety – the very best in publishing today.

For complete information about books available from Penguin – including Puffins, Penguin Classics and Arkana – and how to order them, write to us at the appropriate address below. Please note that for copyright reasons the selection of books varies from country to country.

In the United Kingdom: Please write to *Dept. EP, Penguin Books Ltd, Bath Road, Harmondsworth, West Drayton, Middlesex UB7 ODA*

In the United States: Please write to *Consumer Sales, Penguin Putnam Inc., P.O. Box 12289 Dept. B, Newark, New Jersey 07101-5289.* VISA and MasterCard holders call 1-800-788-6262 to order Penguin titles

In Canada: Please write to *Penguin Books Canada Ltd, 10 Alcorn Avenue, Suite 300, Toronto, Ontario M4V 3B2*

In Australia: Please write to *Penguin Books Australia Ltd, P.O. Box 257, Ringwood, Victoria 3134*

In New Zealand: Please write to *Penguin Books (NZ) Ltd, Private Bag 102902, North Shore Mail Centre, Auckland 10*

In India: Please write to *Penguin Books India Pvt Ltd, 11 Community Centre, Panchsheel Park, New Delhi 110017*

In the Netherlands: Please write to *Penguin Books Netherlands bv, Postbus 3507, NL-1001 AH Amsterdam*

In Germany: Please write to *Penguin Books Deutschland GmbH, Metzlerstrasse 26, 60594 Frankfurt am Main*

In Spain: Please write to *Penguin Books S. A., Bravo Murillo 19, 1° B, 28015 Madrid*

In Italy: Please write to *Penguin Italia s.r.l., Via Benedetto Croce 2, 20094 Corsico, Milano*

In France: Please write to *Penguin France, Le Carré Wilson, 62 rue Benjamin Baillaud, 31500 Toulouse*

In Japan: Please write to *Penguin Books Japan Ltd, Kaneko Building, 2-3-25 Koraku, Bunkyo-Ku, Tokyo 112*

In South Africa: Please write to *Penguin Books South Africa (Pty) Ltd, Private Bag X14, Parkview, 2122 Johannesburg*

READ MORE IN PENGUIN

A CHOICE OF CLASSICS

Anton Chekhov	**The Duel and Other Stories**
	The Kiss and Other Stories
	The Fiancée and Other Stories
	Lady with Lapdog and Other Stories
	The Party and Other Stories
	Plays (The Cherry Orchard/Ivanov/The Seagull/Uncle Vania/The Bear/The Proposal/A Jubilee/Three Sisters)
Fyodor Dostoyevsky	**The Brothers Karamazov**
	Crime and Punishment
	The Devils
	The Gambler/Bobok/A Nasty Story
	The House of the Dead
	The Idiot
	Netochka Nezvanova
	The Village of Stepanchikovo
	Notes from Underground/The Double
Nikolai Gogol	**Dead Souls**
	Diary of a Madman and Other Stories
Alexander Pushkin	**Eugene Onegin**
	The Queen of Spades and Other Stories
	Tales of Belkin
Leo Tolstoy	**Anna Karenin**
	Childhood, Boyhood, Youth
	A Confession
	How Much Land Does a Man Need?
	Master and Man and Other Stories
	Resurrection
	The Sebastopol Sketches
	What is Art?
	War and Peace
Ivan Turgenev	**Fathers and Sons**
	First Love
	A Month in the Country
	On the Eve
	Rudin
	Sketches from a Hunter's Album

READ MORE IN PENGUIN

A CHOICE OF CLASSICS

Jacob Burckhardt	**The Civilization of the Renaissance in Italy**
Carl von Clausewitz	**On War**
Meister Eckhart	**Selected Writings**
Friedrich Engels	**The Origin of the Family**
	The Condition of the Working Class in England
Goethe	**Elective Affinities**
	Faust Parts One and Two (in two volumes)
	Italian Journey
	Maxims and Reflections
	Selected Verse
	The Sorrows of Young Werther
Jacob and Wilhelm Grimm	**Selected Tales**
E. T. A. Hoffmann	**Tales of Hoffmann**
Friedrich Hölderlin	**Selected Poems and Fragments**
Henrik Ibsen	**Brand**
	A Doll's House and Other Plays
	Ghosts and Other Plays
	Hedda Gabler and Other Plays
	The Master Builder and Other Plays
	Peer Gynt
Søren Kierkegaard	**Fear and Trembling**
	Papers and Journals
	The Sickness Unto Death
Georg Christoph Lichtenberg	**Aphorisms**
Karl Marx	**Capital** (in three volumes)
Karl Marx/Friedrich Engels	**The Communist Manifesto**
Friedrich Nietzsche	**The Birth of Tragedy**
	Beyond Good and Evil
	Ecce Homo
	Human, All Too Human
	Thus Spoke Zarathustra
Friedrich Schiller	**Mary Stuart**
	The Robbers/Wallenstein